Classico

Ancient Peoples and Places

THE
ETRUSCANS

General Editor

DR GLYN DANIEL

Ancient Peoples and Places

THE
ETRUSCANS

Raymond Bloch

79 PHOTOGRAPHS
38 LINE DRAWINGS
AND 3 MAPS

New York
FREDERICK A. PRAEGER

THIS IS VOLUME SEVEN IN THE SERIES

Ancient Peoples and Places

GENERAL EDITOR: DR GLYN DANIEL

BOOKS THAT MATTER *This is a revised and expanded
version of* LE MYSTERE ETRUSQUE
Translated by Stuart Hood
© *Club Francais du Livre Paris 1956*
*Published in the United States of America
in 1958 by Frederick A. Praeger, Inc.,
Second impression 1960
Publishers, 15 West 47th Street,
New York 36, N.Y.*
All rights reserved
Library of Congress Catalog Card Number: 58-8176
Printed in Great Britain

CONTENTS

ILLUSTRATIONS

Foreword

IT WAS IN THE COURSE of archaeological work, which has been in progress for about ten years now in Southern Etruria, near the picturesque little town of Bolsena, that this book was first conceived and in part written. Nothing brings one into closer contact with an extinct civilisation or a vanished people than the systematic exploration of its soil. Excavation is, in the last analysis, historical research, and from soil which has been dug with due thoroughness and patience, there emerge not only monuments and objects of different periods, but also a clearer and more definite vision of the birth and evolution of the people who created them.

In writing this Foreword, my thoughts therefore turn to the collaborators and friends who so gallantly participated in the long and often difficult work of research and have contributed to it support and advice; it is to them that I wish to express my gratitude which their efforts and their friendship have so richly earned.

R. B.

Introduction

OF ALL THE PEOPLES of antiquity, the Etruscans today occupy a very special place in our eyes. Their long history on the soil of the Italian peninsula began in the early years of the 7th century B.C. and came to an end only a very short time before the Christian era. At war, first against the Greeks, with whom they disputed the hegemony of the Mediterranean, then against the Romans, who were compelled to fight hard before subjugating them, the Etruscans occupy a place of considerable importance in the works of authors in both the Greek and Latin tongues. Their name, which once inspired such fear, occurs constantly in the Annals of Livy; and Virgil, in his epic description of the origins of Rome, makes a point of relating in broad outline the exploits of the dashing horsemen of ancient Tuscany. Even today, traces of Etruscan cities and burial grounds are very numerous in Umbria, Tuscany and Latium. Over the centuries, chance discoveries and organised excavations have brought to light an immense number of objects of all kinds—sculptures, paintings and products of the minor arts—deriving from the studios and workshops of Etruria. These objects are now the pride and glory of private collections and museums in both Europe and America.

But in spite of the evocative power of these relics, which conjure up out of the darkness aspects of a highly developed but now extinct civilisation, in spite of all this evidence provided by its plastic art, which is both of great historical interest and of rare artistic value, Etruria still presents scientists and laymen alike with a mysterious and obscure phenomenon. Nor do centuries of patient attempts and persistent efforts appear to have succeeded so far in penetrating the veil of mystery behind which she shelters.

Several enigmas certainly combine to give to these first inhabitants of Tuscany a strange and secret air. Where did they come from? What language did they speak? These essential questions have not yet been resolved and give rise to the most varied and contradictory theses. The vexed problem of the origins of Etruria has for long been discussed. Even in antiquity, views on the subject were divided. There was, it is true, general support for the traditional thesis developed in his alert and clear style by Herodotus. For him, it was emigration by sea that brought the Etruscans from Anatolian Lydia and elsewhere in Asia Minor to the sunny shores of the Tyrrhenian sea. This Asiatic origin is accepted without hesitation by the great majority of ancient authors. But Dionysius of Halicarnassus, a Greek rhetorician, who lived in Rome in the times of Augustus, refused to share this general opinion and maintained that the Etruscan people was autochthonous. The discussion continues down to the present time, and we shall see later how the problem is viewed today.

The deciphering of the Etruscan language is an equally difficult and vexed question. In spite of centuries of persistent attempts—admittedly sometimes unsystematic and over bold, but frequently carried out by men of great knowledge and levelheadedness—no solution has been found to the enigma still presented by a language which stands curiously alone among the ancient tongues. In this instance, too, we shall have to sum up present research and to show the deep-seated reasons for what is apparently one of the most astonishing failures of modern linguistic studies.

It is just these difficulties and obscurities that frequently strike the imagination of the general public, which is surprised to see science—in spite of all its progress—marking time for so long; but they must not be allowed to distract attention from the fundamentals of Etruscology—namely the history and civilisation of the Etruscan people. Etruscan history and Etruscan

civilisation, which were so important for the working out of
the fate of Western civilisation in antiquity, are not, in their
general outline, surrounded by obscurity or mystery. Greek
and Latin texts relating to the ancient Tuscans and, above all,
the admirable documentation provided by objects disinterred
either by a freak of chance or through the efforts of archaeologists, allow us to form a broad view of their civilisation;
while some areas are less clearly defined than others, such a
view does bring to life a whole nation with its political and
social organisation, its economy, its religious beliefs and its
artistic creations. It is the purpose of this book, first to make a
frank analysis of the nature of the unsolved problems, and then
to describe the fascinating history of ancient Etruria and to
study in succession the different aspects of the civilisation of the
Etruscan people, their public and private life, their religion
and their art. We shall thus be in a position to acquire an
intimate knowledge of the life of a country and a people which
began to play an important part in the history of the West at
the beginning of the 7th century B.C., and which was conquered by Rome only at the cost of long and bitter wars. Even
after Etruria fell under the onslaughts of the Roman legions
towards the middle of the 3rd century B.C., her cultural rôle
was not cut short. Etruscan workshops continued production
on Tuscan territory until the middle of the 1st century B.C.;
as for Etruscan religious teachings as practised by the *haruspices*,
the Romans made use of them until the fall of the Empire,
when Graeco-Roman paganism itself finally gave way to
triumphant Christianity. As regards the vast problems presented by the civilisation of Etruria—a civilisation which was
originally independent and later subjugated by the Romans—
or by her legacy, to be traced in the life of Rome itself, the work
of archaeologists and historians has made a constant contri-
bution by way of positive knowledge and elucidation, which
enable us to assess ancient traditions and to fill in a number of

gaps. This is the result of centuries of vast historical labours devoted to one of the nations concerned in opening up the Italian peninsula—and thereby the Western world—to a civilisation of which we are the remote beneficiaries. I believe that if we wish to evaluate the present extent of our positive knowledge, we must retrace the course of Etruscan studies from their first hesitant steps at the beginning of modern times to their full flowering. It is extremely instructive, when dealing with such a complex and difficult subject as that of ancient Etruria, to follow the ancient scholars step by step and to trace their attempts and efforts. In this way methods of work, progressively perfected over the centuries, emerge more clearly, and mistakes made in the past reveal errors of judgment of which even today we must beware. Moreover, the gropings of our distant forebears have, in their naïveté, something peculiarly attractive about them and to write the history of men who have themselves made history is perhaps one of the most fascinating pastimes of the historian.

This book therefore begins with a general historical survey of Etruscology. We shall then deal with the key questions for which modern research has still not found final answers—the problem of the origins of the Etruscan people and of their language. The core of the book will be devoted to the different aspects of Etruscan civilisation and will attempt to recreate, as far as possible, the story of an enquiring people, enamoured of life yet concerned with life after death, a people whom we see in their daytoday activities on the admirable frescoes which cover the damp walls of their sombre tombs.

THE MODERNS AND ETRURIA

CHAPTER I

The History of Etruscology

ALREADY IN ROMAN TIMES scholars turned their attention to the nation which, before Rome itself, had almost succeeded in unifying the peninsula for its own ends. The Tuscan sacred books were translated into Latin and compiled by Tarquinius Priscus, himself of Etruscan origin, in the 1st century B.C. Of this translation there remain only a few passages, all of them brief; these are reproduced in the writings of Seneca, of Pliny the Elder and a few others. The Emperor Claudius, stimulated by his great curiosity as an antiquarian, devoted his attention to Italy's Etruscan past. He was helped in his researches by the archives of the great Tuscan families which his first wife, Urganilla, who came from noble Etruscan stock, must have supplied to him; but in this case, too, the losses, so far as we are concerned, are immense, for we possess none of his writings. In particular, nothing is left of his Etruscan grammar—a truly irreparable loss. However, the interest taken by Roman scholarship in the Etruscan people shows that, even in antiquity, they were surrounded by that aura of mystery which has never left them. We can say today that Etruria was rediscovered in the 18th century—but that does not mean that, until then, it was completely neglected by scholars or that there had not been a large number of discoveries on Tuscan soil before that time.

Fundamentally, however, people were interested only in Rome itself, which was the object of passionate study during the Renaissance; the picturesque regions of Tuscany were merely a setting for the products of poetic imagination. But Etruscan tombs, opened up by chance during work in the fields did attract the attention of artists, who sometimes visited them in order to find sources of inspiration. Etruscan frescoes,

now no longer extant, must have served as models for Michelangelo when he drew the head of Aita covered with a wolf's
skin. Aita is no other than the Hades of the Etruscan World
of the Dead. Splendid examples of Etruscan art came to light
by chance. The famous Capitoline wolf was already known in
the Middle Ages; the 16th century saw in succession the discovery, in 1553, of the Arezzo Chimaera; in 1554, of the
Arezzo Minerva; and in 1556, of the statue traditionally called
the *Arringatore*—the Orator. Today these three great bronzes
are still the glory of the Archaeological Museum in Florence.
In the 17th century, some of Tarquinia's frescoed tombs amazed
their discoverers—for instance in 1699, there was the Tartaglia
Tomb and the Tomb of the Cardinal, named respectively after
a lawyer named Tartaglia and Cardinal Garampi, Bishop of
Tarquinia, who were the first to enter these subterranean
dwellings of the dead. In actual fact, the book that was to
give the initial impulse to a movement of passionate interest in
Tuscany was written between 1660 and 1690 by a Scottish
scholar, Sir Thomas Dempster. This is a large work, com-
prising seven volumes, and entitled *De Etruria regali libri
septem*. It is the fruit of vast erudition and fertile imagination,
but it remained in manuscript for over a hundred years. It was
not published in Florence until 1723–24.

Plate 51

Dempster, an admirable connoisseur of ancient literature,
attempted to draw a picture of the history of the ancient
Tuscans, basing himself principally on texts. His study was
illustrated by a fine series of ninety-three plates reproducing
various Etruscan documents. The Florentine senator, Buona-
rotti, followed up these plates with *explicationes* and *conjecturae*,
to illustrate this, the first modest *corpus* of the monuments of
Etruria. Such was the starting point for archaeological and
historical research in Tuscany.

These investigations very quickly fell under three closely
interrelated heads: excavations in the field; the setting up of

Fig. 1. Frieze from the Grotta del Cardinale. *A deceased woman being borne to Hell by winged genii. After an engraving by Byres in* Hypogea of Tarquinia, *part II, pl. 8*

collections of Etruscan objects; and theoretical works dealing with these collections or with general historical questions.

The first excavations worthy of the name began in 1728 on the splendid site of Volterra in the extreme north of Tuscany. In 1739, the tomb of the illustrious Cecina family was brought to light, and in it were found some forty urns, which formed the nucleus of the Volterra Archaeological Museum. This museum was founded about 1750 by the Abbe Mario Guarnacci, whose name it still bears. This was the beginning of the thorough examination of the site, one of the most beautiful and picturesque in the whole of Tuscany. Volterra, in Etruscan *Velathri*, stretched along an escarped hill which dominated the Cecina valley. The extent of the remains of the Etruscan walls indicate that the modern town was less important than the Etruscan 'Lucumony'. There still exists today, together with important portions of the outer wall, the Etruscan gate known as the 'Porta del Arco', which is ornamented with the sculptured heads of divinities. Numerous 18th-century engravers used these magnificent architectural remains for their drawings.

As always in Etruria, the tombs were situated outside the walls. It was an absolute rule in antiquity that the habitations of the dead should be separated from those of the living. Unfortunately, one part of the plateau, on the side of which the tombs were excavated, has been subsiding for centuries because of gigantic landslides. Thus the ancient necropolis of Volterra has been almost completely destroyed. And the Guarnacci Museum, though still one of the richest local museums in Tuscany, has collected predominantly objects of the Hellenistic period.

Of this material the most distinctive part consists of funerary urns in terra-cotta or alabaster. Alabaster was employed by Tuscan artisans only in this region. The lids of these urns carry the reclining figure of the deceased. The sides of the urns are decorated with scenes in relief showing episodes of daily life or of Etrusco-Greek mythology; generally they are included as funerary symbols. This explains the constant recurrence of scenes of departure and of travel on these bas-reliefs. The traveller, who is shown about to leave on foot or in a vehicle for an unknown destination, is none other than the deceased calmly setting out to enter the sombre kingdom of Hades. The wonderful commentaries by Franz Cumont, the eminent historian of religion, on the funerary symbolism of the Romans, might be extended and applied to this vast series of funerary urns. When they discovered documents of this kind, the early 18th-century excavators found themselves faced with productions typically Etruscan both in style and religious significance.

At the same time, a chance discovery at Palestrina, the ancient *Preneste*, situated about 25 miles east of Rome, revealed one of the ancient masterpieces of engraving on bronze, the Ficoroni coffer—today, the pride of the Etruscan Museum in the Villa Guilia at Rome. It was in 1738 that the antiquarian, Francesco Ficoroni, discovered in the soil of this ancient Latin-Etruscan city a great cylindrical bronze coffer with admirable engraved decorations on its lid and sides, representing, he was delighted to discover, the various episodes of the myth of the Argonauts. The ship Argo, 'The Speedy One', carrying the group of daring navigators, has dropped anchor

*Fig. 2. Bas-reliefs decorating the front of a sarcophagus at Volterra; 2nd century B.C.
Ulysses tempted by the sirens*

in Bithynia, in the land of the Bebryces. The vessel has been
pulled ashore and a youth is leaving it, carrying pails and
vases which he is to fill at a nearby spring. The king of the
land, Amycos, was wont to challenge to a boxing match
anyone who had the audacity to set foot on his soil. Being
endowed with exceptional strength, he put them savagely to
death. Pollux has accepted the challenge, has won and is
tying his vanquished enemy to a tree. He still carries on his
hands the *cestus* which he used in the fight. It would be difficult
to imagine a more noble composition or more elegant draughtsmanship. Francesco Ficoroni had had the luck to find the
Etruscan masterpiece which most strongly evokes—admittedly
at a late date, for the coffer dates only from about 330 B.C.—the
spirit of Hellenic classicism.

In short, the soil of Tarquinia continued to reveal both by chance and as a result of several organised surveys, painted funerary chambers. In the middle of the 18th century, a modest worker in this field, Father Gian Nicola Forlivesi, a native of Tarquinia, explored some frescoed tombs in the neighbour-hood of Corneto and left a manuscript on the subject, which was unfortunately lost. However, we find references to it in the writings of the period. But, here as elsewhere, we had to wait for the beginning of the 19th century for research of greater scope to bring to light the jewels of Tuscan art.

One discovery followed another at varying intervals, the result rather of chance than of methodical research. Of much greater importance for the future of Etruscology was the exploitation of new documents. They were exploited in two ways: certain of the big museums where to this day the most important collections of Etruscan art are housed, were founded, and books concerning the products of this art increased in number. We have seen that the Museo Civico at Volterra was set up at that time. It was not its founder, Guarnacci, but the Florentine, Anton Francesco Gori, who speedily published an account of the Volterra collections. This study was con-tained in what was, for the period, a considerable work, which Gori himself published between 1737 and 1740, and which bore the title *Museum Etruscum exhibens insignia veterum Etrus-corum Monumenta*. This 'Etruscan Museum' consists of three large folios. The text is very uneven in quality, but was accom-panied by three hundred illustrations, reproducing not only what was already a considerable number of Etruscan works of art, but also, it must be admitted, Greek and Roman works erroneously considered to be Etruscan. These three beautiful volumes do honour to one of the pioneers of Etruscology. Moreover, the uncertainty of the attributions of his judgment must not lead us to underestimate the seriousness of the study or the careful execution and beauty of the engravings. In

Fig. 3. The discovery of the Tomb of the Typhon. After an engraving by Byres in
Hypogea of Tarquinia, *part I, pl. 4*

particular, Gori gives a summary of Forlivesi's manuscript on
the discovery of Tarquinian frescoes. This is the only evidence
we have for some of them today. Tarquinia also attracted the
attention of painters and engravers—some of them famous
ones. James Byres, an English painter who was a friend of
Piranesi, made a number of sketches showing what the tombs
looked like at the time of their discovery. These were not
published in London until 1842 under the title '*Hypogaei*' *or
the sepulchral caverns of Tarquinia*. Piranesi himself, as we shall
see, was interested in the cemeteries at Cortona.

Figs. 1, 3, 6, 19

But other collections were formed and new museums opened.
The centre of what has been called '*Etruscheria*'—the Etruscomania of the 18th century, that excessive enthusiasm for

Etruscan art and civilisation which it is worth while to recall in detail here—was situated in the heart of Tuscany, at Cortona, a little picturesque town on top of a hill richly clad in olive groves and vineyards. It was there that the Cortona Etruscan Academy was set up on December 29, 1726—an institution whose frequently haphazard activity has, in its naïve zeal, something rather pleasing about it. This society pursued its investigations throughout the 18th century and included the greatest names in Italy and abroad. A museum and library were the tangible manifestations of its activity. Once again, it is to Anton Francesco Gori's credit that he published, without delay, a survey of the collections assembled in that small Italian provincial museum. His *Museum Cortonense* is the companion volume to his study of the Volterra Museum. Here, as at Volterra, and as later on in Florence, the investigations of 18th-century learned societies ran parallel to the organisation of collections of antiquities. We find here an intimate link between archaeology and the emergence of the study of ancient history, and this close bond remains one of the great laws governing research in that sphere.

How curious was the fate of this local society, whose memory lives on in Tuscany. Cortona, the famous royal seat of ancient Tuscany, the town which, after the strife of the Middle Ages, gave birth to the most celebrated of its sons, Luca Signorelli, creator of the admirable frescoes in Orvieto Cathedral, richly deserved to be the cradle of the Etruscan Renaissance. On August 29, 1726 the Abbé Onofrio Baldelli, assisted by three of his relatives, founded the Etruscan Academy, which was to advance so greatly the history of antiquity. A pleasing feature of its activities was the evocation of Etruscan names and ancient Etruscan customs. Every year, the Academy elected a President who was given the name of *lucumon* or king. The Academy itself was composed of one hundred and forty members, of whom forty were citizens of Cortona, the rest from outside the town. Their meetings were called *Le Notti Coritane*—'The Cortona Nights'—nights that were, however, given over to study. The bells of the town hall called the Academicians together twice a month, and ladies of the nobility were invited to participate. At these meetings, letters and communications were read; newly discovered antique objects were presented, and members engaged in courteous discussion on the most burning problems of the day.

This activity continued throughout the century and resulted in nine fine volumes, published 1738–95. It is a great pleasure to turn over the pages of the elegant quarto tomes, which bear the noble title of *Saggi di Dissertazioni accademiche pubblicamente lette nella nobile accademia etrusca dell'antichissima città di Cortona.* The texts of these communications are pleasingly illustrated by good engravings and the subjects treated are most varied. Not all of them concern Etruria; monuments in Rome and in Asia Minor are described by travellers and scholars and certain articles deal with broad questions of religious history, such as one on the worship in antiquity of sacred woods, or *nemora*.

Plate 68

Two of the greatest scholars of the century devoted part of their writings to the history and the art of the Etruscans—the Comte de Caylus and Winckelmann. Winckelmann's *History of Art*, like the *Recueil des Antiquités* of the Comte de Caylus, contain chapters devoted to ancient Tuscany. The former naturally is chiefly concerned to incorporate Etruscan art in the vast system he had conceived of the evolution of ancient art; the Comte de Caylus, for his part, limits himself to the publication and analysis of various monuments which he had seen or of which he was the owner. It is not unimportant that these two excellent minds were not afraid to tackle the difficult problem of ancient Etruria, and we shall see in a moment where their methods fall into place and the nature of their conclusions. As for Piranesi, although his heart was captivated by Rome with its innumerable and miraculous antiquities, he knew and studied Tuscany; it will be of interest to recall later a relatively little known debate on Etruria in which he had as opponent a French scholar, Mariette.

This heroic period of Etruscology concludes with the works of the Abbé Luigi Lanzi. The Abbé Lanzi, who was born in 1732 and died in 1812, devoted a life of zealous study and labour to various questions posed by Etruscan history. He shared the errors of his time, but in his analysis of the various specimens and the conclusions he drew from them, he showed that he had a mind less prone to flights of fancy than most of his predecessors. Both archaeologist and linguist, he is an epitome of the knowledge of his century, but he also made new contributions to problems long debated. Florentine by birth, he spent the greater part of his life in his native city, and Umberto Segre paid sympathetic homage about half a century ago to his courageous life in a book entitled *Luigi Lanzi e le sue opere*. It is only right that modern scholars should grant to their remote predecessors the place they deserve in the history of the first hesitating steps and early progress of their science.

In 1789 the Abbé Lanzi published a work of three volumes which, at last, defined the place of the Etruscan language amongst the ancient Italic dialects. His *Saggio di lingua etrusca e di altre lingue antiche d'Italia* is in fact a *summa* of the knowledge of the period, not only with regard to the language, but also to the institutions, history and art of the Etruscans. This book constitutes a turning point in the history of Etruscology. Assisted by his pupil, Zannoni, the Abbé Lanzi undertook to arrange an Etruscan collection at the Uffizi in Florence. This collection was the beginning of the Florence Archaeological Museum, founded as recently as in 1870. Finally, one of his books was the first to demonstrate systematically the Greek origin of the majority of the painted vases, found on Italian soil, which were traditionally ascribed to the Etruscan civilisation.

But we must ask the fundamental question concerning the method used in these epigraphic and archaeological works. How was research conducted at the time, and what is the reason for crass errors—or so they seem to us—committed by so many distinguished minds? What, on the other hand, were the definitive advances made by these pioneers of Etruscology and how far in the end did their efforts advance science?

In attempting to resolve these fascinating questions we must have a clear idea of the state of historical and archaeological knowledge concerning ancient Tuscany at the beginning of the 18th century. Basically, this knowledge reduced itself to the information handed down by the writers of antiquity. The Scotsman Dempster assembled it and attempted to exploit it in his *De Etruria regali*. But these interpretations were the work of a powerful but too daring imagination, and their author's vast erudition mixed in hopeless confusion accurate fact, baseless opinion and wild speculation. Such a state of knowledge on every aspect of Etruria was inevitable; archaeology was as yet in its infancy. To us today it is clear that the essential core of solid knowledge we are able to acquire of the Etruscan people, whose language remains barely understood and who have, moreover, left us no literary texts, must be based on the detailed study of the pictorial documents provided by their art.

Even now Etruscan archaeology, perhaps more than any other, presents certain extremely difficult problems. The Etruscans were not a creative people comparable to the ancient Greeks—or at least, they required outside influences in order to create. These impulses came, first from the Near East, then from Hellas itself. It is therefore impossible to understand and to follow the different periods of Etruscan art without constant reference to the impact of Hellenic models. Etruscan artists responded to these models in a manner that varied according to time and place; their vision of the world is none the less personal for that, and frequently very strange. But the question of influence and prototypes cannot be neglected in a frank analysis of their art.

Let us now consider the unhappy situation in which the 18th-century Etruscologist must have found himself. Greek art was still very little known. True, travellers were beginning to visit Greece and the Near East. But Greek archaeological knowledge was still slight and vague. It would have been impossible, in these conditions, to arrive at a sound appreciation of artistic objects brought to light from time to time in Tuscany, first by chance and later, through excavation. Indispensable points of comparison were lacking, and this fact weighed heavily against the progress of Etruscological research. It also explains in part the mistakes of this naïve *Etruscheria*. Moreover, some of the difficulties encountered by our remote predecessors still face us today. Confronted with certain bronzes found in Etruria, we ask ourselves whether they should be considered Etruscan works of art or Greek ones; and the debate over some of the most famous bronzes of antique origin, such as the Arezzo Chimaera, is not yet at an end. In the 18th century the uncertain knowledge of Hellenic art and the lack of familiarity with Tuscan production led to fundamental misconceptions. Etruscan tombs often contain a large number of Greek imported vases, and Vulci—dug systematically from the beginning of the 18th century onwards —has furnished more pieces of Attic black figure ware than the soil of Athens itself, thanks to the protective roofs of the Tuscan tombs, which were dug out of the tufa of the Maremma or the foothills of the Appenines. Eighteenth-century amateurs and scholars long believed that this vast collection of Greek vases which they saw emerging from the soil of Tuscany or Campania, was Etruscan. Minute analytical labours were necessary to rectify this misconception.

Thus, the ignorance and the doubts of the period under discussion can be explained by the tentative state of archaeology and science; but we must undoubtedly add to these another reason, this time springing from national psychology. Italy was divided, and in the North dominated by Austria. Quite naturally she sought in her past history some sort of compensation for her humiliated *amour propre*. The period of the Risorgimento was still far off, but national aspirations already existed. Thus, there arose a tendency to over-estimate the past of the peninsula and, above all, of the Etruscan civilisation, the earliest to spring up on Italian soil. The Italian people loved to exalt the glories of their past. This is one of the deep reasons for the Etruscomania that held sway until the day when, thanks to the advance of the French armies, Lombardy and Milan were liberated.

But we must examine in greater detail the attitude of individual men, for it differed greatly from one person to the next. Although imagination often won the day, the spirit of scientific observation, which was to be the basis of the advances made in the following centuries, was already apparent. Admittedly this scientific spirit does not manifest itself in the archaeological research conducted in the field. This was still in its infancy. Objects without artistic value were neglected. No inventory of excavations was kept—a fact which today greatly hampers the study of evidence brought to light at the time. We shall have to wait until the second half of the 19th or even the beginning of the present century, for the gradual emergence, thanks chiefly to the work of the prehistorians, of the fundamental principles of archaeological research—principles based on a careful survey of the terrain and the stratigraphical study of the soil.

Temperamental differences become very apparent in the examination of existing evidence and the conclusions arrived at from it. Some had no respect for the truth when analysing fact; others, on the contrary, showed a reserve and prudence worthy of true scientists. Among the former we must place

Guarnacci, the founder of the Volterra Museum. As we read his three volumes entitled *Origini italiche ossiano Memorie istorico-Etrusche sopra l'antichissimo regno d'Italia* (Lucca, 1767–72), we pass from pedantic erudition to the most daring and quite obviously false conclusions. According to Guarnacci, the Etruscans were not only the cultural vanguard of all other Italic peoples, but also, at certain periods, ahead of the Greeks. At about the same time, there appeared in Rome several volumes by Giovanni Battista Passeri, entitled *Picturae Etruscorum in vasculis primum in unum collectae*. In them Passeri describes an admirable collection of Greek and Italic vases, from around Chiusi and Naples, which were at that time owned by Cardinal Gualtieri. Subsequently, the collection passed to the Vatican Library and today constitutes the nucleus of the extremely rich collection of painted vases in the Gregorian Etruscan Museum. Passeri believed that these vases, imported from Greece or of Greek manufacture, were Etruscan products and the subjects represented on them connected with the funerary beliefs of the ancient Etruscans. His entire analysis and interpretation are thus falsified from the start. Of his work, which bears the mark of obvious Etruscomania, nothing remains valid, though the vast collection of documents, it is true, proved useful for the researches of his successors. The engravings of the period are often fanciful and inexact. These somewhat free interpretations, however, are not entirely devoid of value or charm.

But better minds were probing the Etruscan question. About 1770–75 the famous engraver, Gian Battista Piranesi, and the Frenchman Mariette were opponents in a very lively debate concerning the value of Etruscan art and its influence on Rome. This quarrel is a good illustration of the bitterness the clash of two distinguished minds, both of which were attempting a synthesis, could engender at a period when the basic material had not yet been assembled. In 1761, Piranesi, who proudly bore the title *Socius antiquariorum regiae societatis ludi-nensis*—Fellow of the Society of Antiquaries of London—published his great work *Della magnificenza ed architettura dei Romani*. Forty illustrations or vignettes accompanied an impor-tant text of 212 folio pages, which set out to illustrate the splendour of the Latin genius and of Rome. These pages, as Monsieur Focillon has said in his fine book on Piranesi, are full of burning passion. In them Piranesi, as an artist and as a man inspired, defends Latin civilisation with all his soul. At this period certain denigrators of ancient Rome alleged that, before the conquest of Greece, the Romans were completely ignorant in the art of building. Piranesi has recourse to Latin texts and Roman archaeological remains to reconstruct the Rome of the Tarquins. To this we owe a number of admirable illustrations of the Cloaca Maxima, the sewer dating from the Etrusco-Roman dynasty, which had, in part, survived the centuries. The problem of the origins of Roman art leads him to study Etruscan influences on Rome. His conclusion is this: Roman architecture was born on Italian soil; it is national; it is indigenous; it owes everything, not to Greek art, but to the architecture of the Etruscans. And he produces one engraving after another, showing us the plan and the decoration of the Etruscan temple according to Vitruvius, or attempts to recon-struct that temple.

These engravings are very beautiful, but they are not free from error. In the tripartite temple, the plan of which is traced according to Vitruvius, Piranesi puts the three *cellae*, sheltering the statues of the Gods, along one of the sides of the sanctuary, whereas, in reality, they opened directly on to the back of the *naos*. The roof is drawn with extreme care. Sharing a view which was very prevalent at this time, Piranesi believes that Etruscan art was derived from that of the Egyptians. Yet, there is more than a grain of truth in the relationship he estab-lishes between the Etruscans and the art of ancient Rome.

C

This defence of a national art of ancient Italy brought forward an opponent in the person of a distinguished French art-lover, Pierre Jean Mariette. He, although an admirer of Piranesi, found the rôle allotted by the latter to the Greeks in the development of Roman art too insignificant. In his view, it was Greece that exercised the influence on Rome which Piranesi ascribes to the Etruscans. Mariette expressed his opinion firmly in a letter addressed to the *Gazette Littéraire de l'Europe*, published in a supplement to that Gazette on Sunday, November 4, 1764. A similar difference in points of view exists between certain scholars to this day. For it is extremely difficult in these complex questions to get at the truth if, instead of using a delicately balanced judgment, one attempts to decide difficult problems by drastic formulae—formulae that are as a rule partly false. Mariette is no exception to this rule when he writes: 'Signor Piranesi maintains that when the first Romans wished to erect massive buildings, the solidity of which astonishes us, they were obliged to enlist the assistance of Etruscan architects who were their neighbours. One might as well say "the assistance of the Greeks", for the Etruscans, who were Greek by origin, were ignorant of the arts and practised only those of them which had been taught to their fathers in the land of their origin.' A mistaken reflection, though we do seem to meet it again in certain contemporary writings.

The dispute between Piranesi and Mariette did not stop there. Piranesi, who was offended by his opponent's remarks, answered him rather pointedly in *Osservazioni*, which he published in his turn. He rightly attacks his opponent's daring assertion that the Etruscans were Greeks. And he criticises his excessive lack of appreciation of Roman art, which Mariette treats simply as corrupt Greek art.

This quarrel was important in the history of Etruscology, for the personalities of the two opponents directed the attention of the general public towards the fundamental problem of the origin of the Etruscans. Meanwhile, Piranesi, motivated by the complex feelings of archaeologist and Italian patriot, continued to be interested in the vestiges of Tuscan art. And he went both to Cortona and to Chiusi to copy on the spot the friezes decorating the walls of several tombs. In a work published in 1765, entitled *Della introduzione e del progresso delle Belle Arti in Europa nei tempi antichi,* he again refers to certain fundamental ideas which had guided him in his dispute with Mariette. Several illustrations in this new book reproduce geometrical designs copied by him from the painted friezes in recently opened tombs at Tarquinia and Chiusi. Piranesi's interpretation seems rather fanciful, and different elements, from different tombs, are grouped on the same plate. The lack of exact indication of their origin and mistaken interpretation rob his work of a great deal of documentary value.

One cannot fail to be interested in the methods of the most famous scholars of their time, Winckelmann and the Comte de Caylus. However, Winckelmann who exercised an extraordinary influence on the movement of ideas and on art in his time, did not, either in his life or in his works, show any real interest in Etruscan archaeology or art. He did not make use, in his extensive writings, of the Etruscan collections which were being assembled at Florence, at Cortona and at Volterra. Nor did he make any use of Gori's voluminous publications. This lack of interest and his almost excessive tendency to synthesis make the pages he devotes to Etruscan art rather poor, in spite of the vigour of his intellect. There are hardly any correct observations, but only attempts at synthesis and rather hasty over-all views. He had, however, the great merit of grasping and stating the fact that, contrary to the opinion accepted in his time, most vases found in Etruscan tombs and in the soil of Campania and Sicily were Greek and not Etruscan. But it was to fall to the Abbé Lanzi to demonstrate this fact scientifically.

The impression we have from looking through the *Recueil d'antiquités égyptiennes, grecques, etrusques et romaines*, published in Paris by the Comte de Caylus in 1752, is different. True, Caylus, when dealing with the question of Etruscan art, is confronted by the same difficulties as his contemporaries. But he is more careful than Winckelmann and what he writes of antiques which he either possessed or may have seen is solid and accurate. He admits his ignorance and a reflection such as follows is that of a true scholar: 'In this field,' he writes, 'one must often have the courage not to know and not to blush at an admission which does one more honour than the pom-pous display of useless erudition.' He understands the value and the necessity of comparing objects which are similar, or which belong to the same series. An observation such as this is still valid: 'I wish that the evidence of the documents were more frequently supplemented by the comparative method, which is for the antiquarian, what observation and experiment are for the physician.' And in his wisdom, he returns to the same idea when he regrets that only too often he is unable to decide whether a certain object should be attributed to the Egyptians, the Greeks or the Etruscans: 'We are not in a position to distinguish the products of these different peoples, we have not enough objects for comparison.'

This same spirit of observation and judgment enabled the Abbé Lanzi to refute an error deeply rooted in the Etrusco-mania of his time, whereby all the painted vases discovered on Italian soil were attributed to the Etruscans. The three disser-tations which he published in France in 1806 under the title *Dei vasi antichi dipinti volgarmente chiamati etruschi* enable us to distinguish in him the same intellectual honesty as in the Comte de Caylus. The importance of these conclusions is great, since for the first time a definite, although still somewhat incomplete, distinction is made between Greek and Etruscan pottery, and this work may be considered the point of departure

of modern science. The Abbé Lanzi had to fight against a
very ancient prejudice, shared by the greatest minds. Did not
Goethe, full of enthusiasm, write in his *Italienische Reise* which
appeared in 1787: 'A very high price is now paid for Etruscan
vases . . . There isn't a traveller who does not wish to possess
one . . .' Thus the Abbé states, not without melancholy,
'*Non vi é errore piu difficile a sterminare di quello che a radice in una
falsa nomenclatura.*' There is no error more difficult to eradicate
than that which is rooted in a false terminology. A badly given
name, continues the Abbé, is like a counterfeit coin in circu-
lation. Even if considered false in one country, it continues to
circulate in another.

However, he set about courageously to destroy the opinion
of the *Etruscomanes* of his time by the careful analysis of the art
of the vases he examined, and also by the study of their
inscriptions. Why, said this scholar, should we attribute to
the Etruscans objects bearing inscriptions in the Greek language? This proof did not immediately find the support it
deserved. The almost incredible quantity of beautiful Attic
vases brought to light by the excavations at the beginning of
the 19th century in the tombs at Vulci, in the very heart of
Tuscany, led to constant talk of Etruscan vases, and *The
Etruscan Vase*, which is the title given by Prosper Mérimée to
one of his most brilliant short stories, must have been a
Greek vase, originating from Greece itself, or from one of the
Greek studios which flourished in southern Italy from the
4th century B.C. onwards. It was not until the second half of
the 19th century that this misconception was finally eradicated.
The discovery, in Greece itself, of vases bearing the same
Greek signatures as the vases brought to light in the Tuscan
tombs, finally demonstrated their true origin.

Lanzi died in 1812. He was buried in the church of Santa
Croce in Florence and a laudatory inscription was engraved
on his tomb. This honour was well deserved. Through his

wide knowledge, which neglected no aspect of Etruscan civilisation, this open-minded scholar, epigraphist and archaeo-logist, had opened the way to modern research.

With the beginning of the 19th century, there opens a new and decisive period in the history of Etruscology. The gropings and errors of the preceding period are replaced by more methodical and more sure scholarship; archaeology and lin-guistics emerge gradually from the fog in which they have been fumbling, and it becomes possible to follow the con-tinuous line of the progress of these disciplines up to our own time. But discoveries are so frequent and works of all kinds so numerous that we must trace their history in general outline; all the aspects of this multiform quest throw a light on the various facets of Etruscan civilisation. Towards 1820 an association of savants of different nationalities was formed round a young scholar called Gerhard, and the Duc de Luynes. The support of Prince Frederick of Prussia made possible the foundation of an Institute destined to have a long and brilliant career, the *Istituto di Correspondenza archaeologica*. The first meeting of this Institute took place on the Capitol on April 21, 1829. It is not without significance that Gerhard, the man who was its moving spirit, directed his attention and his interest to the Etruscan world. The works he dedicated to the charming subject of Etruscan mirrors are still used today. During the period which saw the beginning of this new scientific activity, splendid monuments of Tuscan art were brought to light. Several frescoed tombs were found at Tar-quinia, among them, some of the jewels of ancient painting—the Tomb of Bigae and the Tomb of the Baron, discovered in the same year, 1827.

At this happy period for Etruscan archaeology, there began the systematic investigation of tombs whose riches have proved quite inexhaustible. In 1828, in the course of ploughing, a team of oxen caused the ceiling of a tomb in the neighbourhood of Vulci to fall in. This was the beginning of feverish and often clumsy activity, which was given free rein in a district heretofore practically unknown. Lucien Bonaparte, Prince of Canino and owner of a large part of the territory containing the ancient tombs of Vulci, directed this hasty work of exploration which, unfortunately, lacked any care or scientific safeguards. In less than a year his collection of antiquities was enriched by more than two thousand Greek vases. Other private collections were formed simultaneously; that of a rich land-owner in the region, Campanari, was to form the nucleus of the admirable series of Greek vases in the Gregorian Etruscan Museum in the Vatican. We cannot sufficiently deplore the fact, however, that such fruitful excavations should have been carried out quite unmethodically. Interest was shown only in rare and valuable objects; the remainder was left on the spot or destroyed; the tombs were closed up again without even an attempt to make exact drawings of them or an exact inventory of the objects they contained. The harm done by such negligence is now irreparable, and for all the valuable material that has been preserved we lack documentary evidence such as would have been provided by properly kept records of the excavations. Nevertheless, the innumerable objects thus brought to the knowledge of scholars in great quantities rapidly extended their knowledge of Greece and Etruria. They themselves were fully aware of their good fortune; Gerhard's enthusiastic letters are sufficient proof of that.

Plate 12

Faced with these new discoveries, interest was awakened in many quarters, and the most varied monuments emerged from their centuries-old hiding places. It was in 1834 that the beautiful sarcophagus of Adonis was found at Tuscania; in 1835, the great statue of Mars was excavated in the neighbourhood of the Umbrian town of Todi. These two sculptures were to be two of the major pieces in the Exhibition of Etruscan Art and Civilisation which toured Europe in 1955

Plate 70

and 1956. Then, a discovery of capital importance proved that from the middle of the 7th century B.C. Etruria passed through a period of great prosperity. On April 22, 1836, at Cerveteri, the Archpriest Regolini and General Galassi opened up a tomb of unbelievable opulence, whose gold jewellery represents the most accomplished work of the Tuscan goldsmiths. The entire material brought to light proved the close ties which (on the cultural and artistic plane) linked 7th-century Etruria to the countries of the Eastern Mediterranean. The first book dealing with the whole of Etruscan history and using a proper scientific method, appeared about this time: it was the work entitled *Die Etrusker* by Karl Ottfried Muller. Published in 1828, it was re-edited after revision by another scholar Deecke, and in its new form it is still usable. Yet very few scientific books stand the stern test of time. In the first half of the 19th century it was particularly important to gain a greater knowledge of the Tuscan countryside in which many picturesque and out-of-the-way places remained practically unknown to the public. Scholars learnt from accounts of journeys off the beaten track. It was George Dennis, a British consul in Italy, who wrote the most valuable of these accounts of journeys made through districts which were still half-wild. His book, *The Cities and Cemeteries of Etruria*, appeared in 1848 and went into several editions. This success was amply merited, for Dennis, a cultured amateur, contrived to write an account full of life and humour, and to unite the most minute and detailed observation with an amiable and lively style. Even now, there is no better introduction to the study of ancient Etruria than the reading of this little masterpiece; its charm and its value remain undimmed after a century.

Until approximately 1880, a date marking the end of another stage in the history of Etruscology, books and discoveries alternate and multiply. We see vast collections being formed which grouped figured art and other works of art of the same type such as vases, mirrors and funerary urns. Today, these collections require rearrangement for, since that time, the material has been enriched to an extraordinary extent, and the methods of study and exhibition have naturally also been modified. At the present moment, however, these collections are indispensable for research. The inscriptions were grouped in a first *Corpus*, the *Corpus Inscriptionum Italicarum*, by Fabretti, the supplements to which were published as late as 1880 and are still useful.

Major discoveries are legion. In 1857 François discovered at Vulci the monumental tomb with its fresco-covered walls, which was to bear his name. Soon afterwards its paintings were removed from the walls and taken to Rome, to the museum of their owners, the Torlonias. François did not reap the reward for his merits as an excavator, for the harsh climate of Vulci, where malaria was rampant until very recently, cost him his life. A very rich art-lover, the Marchese Campana, formed a collection of antiquities famous for its variety and importance. Etruscan art occupied a considerable place in it. It was, above all, at Cerveteri that his activities were given full rein. Soon, his collection included a vast number of Greek and Etruscan vases, often of great value, and the famous sarcophagus, with two figures lying on their funeral couch, which is now one of the glories of the Louvre. When, after the death of its owner, the enormous collection was dispersed, it enriched a number of European museums, above all the Plates 21-23 Louvre and the Hermitage in Leningrad. A little later, towards 1860, the inexhaustible riches of the necropolis at Cerveteri enabled Castellani, a Roman citizen, to collect a magnificent series of vases of different origins. After his death some went abroad; others were incorporated in the collections of the Roman museums. Between 1855 and 1866 the Barberini family had extensive excavations carried out in the region of Preneste, a town originally Etruscan and then Roman, situated about 25 miles to the east of Rome. Wonderful tombs containing—as does the Regolini-Galassi tomb—treasures of the 7th century B.C. were brought to light. This material may be admired in Rome in the rooms of the Museum of the Villa Giulia and the Pigorini Prehistorical Museum. History could not but profit greatly from this series of discoveries.

One of the discoveries that yielded the most information was made beyond the boundaries of Etruria—at Villanova, about 3 miles north of Bologna, in that region occupied by the Etruscans between the 6th and 4th centuries B.C., when it was known as Etruria Circumpadana. In 1853 Count Gozza-dini brought to light, at the Villanovan site, a necropolis where the rather poor tombs contained vases whose form recalled that of a double truncated cone. Here one was dealing with traces of an Italic civilisation which had preceded Etruscan civilisation itself, and was called 'Villanovan' after the place where it was first discovered. This fact was of prime importance to the historian; and the whole question of the origins of the Etruscans had henceforward to be considered in the light of this discovery.

The point that marks the last stage in the evolution of Etruscological research must be placed about 1870. Since then no factor has greatly modified the direction followed by modern research or its steady progress. The period opened in 1869 with the excavations carried out in the ancient Certosa at Bologna, which revealed the existence of a vast Etruscan necropolis very different from the tombs brought to light a short time before at Villanova. The excavations, conducted by Zannoni, were the first to be carried out in accordance with the strict rules which the archaeologist must respect. Each tomb was carefully described, its material meticulously catalogued and the different layers of the soil, far from being arbitrarily mixed, were scrupulously identified, as they should be if one wishes history to profit from them. Zannoni thus

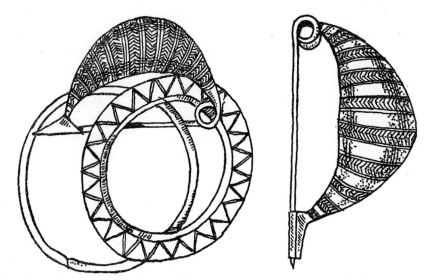

Fig. 4. Bronze fibulae in the form of a leech. Engraved decoration; about 700 B.C. From Capena, Villa Giulia Museum, Rome

gave the first example of modern scientific excavation in an Etruscan tomb.

This example was soon followed, for excavations were intensified throughout Tuscany. In turn, the soil of Tarquinia, Vulci, Chiusi, Vetulonia, Bologna and Orvieto was opened up by the pick of the excavator. The admirable archaic Tombs of Hunting and Fishing, of the Lionesses and the Bulls, were unearthed at Tarquinia between 1873 and 1892. The increasing number of discoveries led to an excellent decision—an official bulletin of Italian excavations, the *Notizie degli scavi*, was founded in 1876; since that date it has appeared regularly every year, furnishing an indispensable mine of information. A department for the organisation and supervision of the antiquities in the peninsula was set up and this made possible a considerable increase in the number of qualified excavators.

Great museums were created: the museum in the Villa Giulia in Rome, which was to house the finds of Southern Etruria and Latium; the Archaeological Museum in Florence, where the material found in the excavations in present-day Tuscany was to be collected; the museums at Bologna, Tarquinia, Chuisi and others. Together with the Gregorian Etruscan Museum in the Vatican, which had already been inaugurated in 1836, the museums in the Villa Giulia and in Florence were destined to house the collections of Etruscan art. Today they represent centres of attraction for anyone interested in the strange and fascinating civilisation of the Etruscan people. The ground floor of the Florence Archaeological Museum is divided into sections which correspond to the ancient centres of Etruria. It is in fact a topographical museum enabling both visitor and scholar to come into successive contact with the various kingships of the Etruscan confederation. It is to Milani, former keeper of the Museum, that credit must go for having arranged his material geographically. His *Museo topographico dell' Etruria* was inaugurated in 1897 and has developed constantly ever since.

The rational organisation of these great Etruscan museums and the setting-up or enlarging of minor museums was all the more beneficial because surveys carried out all over Tuscany have become increasingly numerous. It is not possible to enumerate them in detail here, for the subject is too large and too complex. Let it suffice to recall the succession of major discoveries which, since 1916, have been made around Veii, ten miles north of Rome. Through them we rediscovered, to a great extent, the admirable plastic decoration of the great Veian temple, named after Apollo; there we find a series of
Plates 39-42   terra-cottas of almost life size, of exquisite artistry. Among them an Apollo, undoubtedly the work of the master craftsman Vulca, has quickly acquired well deserved fame. This is a group of great artistic merit.

Town sites also began to be explored—admittedly very timidly. But at last attention was no longer centred exclusively on the necropolis. Thus round about 1890, Brizio explored the interesting city of Marzabotto and the remains of its houses. More recently, the plateau on which stood the holy city of Tarquinii, has been successfully excavated by Monsieur   Plate 59
Romanelli, the present keeper of antiquities of the Forum and the Palatine. The American School in Rome was able, in recent years, to survey the site of ancient Cosa, on the shores of the Tyrrhenian sea; and the French school in Rome received permission in 1946 to survey the area where Volsinii, the capital of the Etruscan confederation, stood. These excavations   Plates 6, 7
have in fact led to the rediscovery of the vanished city and have made possible a survey of its site and its surroundings. We must be grateful to the young Italian republic for having so generously granted to foreign schools permission to excavate. This is valuable proof of a spirit of international understanding and nothing would serve better to strengthen the bonds between the nations than such co-operation in the cultural sphere. It is fortunate that France is thus able to regain in the fields of Etruscology, a place which she seemed at one time to have lost.

Readers will find at the end of this book a list of fundamental works on the basic problems of Etruscan civilisation. These works are, for the most part, relatively recent. Apart from them, a great number of monographs, relating to different Etruscan cities, to various aspects of their life and art have been published. This very flowering of sound publications now permits us to trace a picture of Etruscan history, based on well-tried foundations. A considerable work, begun in 1893, aims at assembling all the epigraphic texts known so far. This is the *Corpus inscriptionum etruscarum* on which many scholars are collaborating. The Institute of Etruscan Studies, which has its seat in Florence and which includes scholars from different countries, serves as a co-ordinating committee for all that concerns ancient Etruria. Since 1927, there has been appearing under its patronage the very important review *Studi etruschi*; it includes among its collaborators specialists in the most varied fields—not only archaeologists and linguists, but also medical men and naturalists. For in order to advance, Science requires the assistance of men who have been trained in what would seem to be quite separate fields.

Plates 1–4

All around us new techniques are developing at a constantly increasing tempo; it would, therefore, be surprising had archaeology—and Etruscan archaeology in particular—which is constantly at grips with the physical world in its search for the past, not also had recourse to recently perfected scientific methods.

Here we will deal only with the application to Etruscological research of new methods invented or developed by the Italian expert, C. M. Lerici. I had the personal pleasure of watching Signor Lerici at work in the tomb area at Cerveteri in April, 1957. Quite apart from the general principles which apply to all systematic excavations, one of his methods of investigation is based on electrical data. The principle is a simple one. The earth is a conductor of electricity, but its degree of conductivity varies according to the nature of the rocks which compose the earth's crust. The presence of terraces, walls, ditches, roads, tombs and wells in a given area changes the conductivity of the rocks which compose the earth's crust: this is revealed by potentiometers. The irregularities in the readings of these instruments allow a technician to locate very precisely the ruins he is looking for.

As far as I am aware, it was an English scholar, R. J. C. Atkinson of Edinburgh University, who first applied this method to archaeology. At Cerveteri, Lerici, using an improved model, discovered a large number of tombs, which have yielded important Etrusco-Greek finds, in an area which had already been thoroughly searched. He has also perfected a method of deciding, before an excavation is even started, whether it is really worth while and, if so, how to set about it. The method can be applied only to chamber tombs. An electric borer allows a hole of about ten centimetres in diameter to be made on the exact site of the tomb, piercing earth, rock and the roof of the tomb itself. A small electrically operated camera with a flashlight and remote control—like those used by agents in the war—is then inserted in a metallic cylinder which is provided with a window. The length of the cylinder can be regulated and it can be used up to a depth of about 20 feet. The whole apparatus is then introduced into the borehole. By means of the remotely controlled flashlight one can then photograph the walls of the tomb. Gradual rotation of the cylinder allows the perimeter of the chamber to be covered with twelve shots. They record precisely the contents of the tomb, say whether it has been violated or not, and indicate whether it is worth excavating. The photograph also reveals the exact location of the entrance corridor. Furnished with all the data he requires, the archaeologist can then begin his work under the best conditions.

This brings us to the end of this rapid journey into the past of Etruscology. It becomes clear that our own efforts are merely a sequel to those of innumerable scholars who, down the centuries, were obsessed by the idea of penetrating the mystery of a nation which appears to have set the stage for the great adventure of Rome. We must now give an idea of the state of our knowledge and point without complacency both to the gaps in it and to its achievements. What do we know of the origins and the language of the Tuscan people? These will be the first two questions we shall attempt to answer.

PART TWO

THE TWO ASPECTS OF
THE ETRUSCAN 'MYSTERY'

CHAPTER II

The Origins of the Etruscan People

IN THE EYES of both the ancient and the modern world the
Etruscans have always appeared a strange people who did
not have much in common with the populations who were
their neighbours. Quite naturally, therefore, both have attempted to discover what their true origins might be. This is
a delicate and difficult problem—and one for which no
universally accepted solution has yet been found. How do
matters stand at present? To answer this question it is important
to recall the views of ancient writers on the subject as well as
the subsequent judgments of modern scholars. In this way we
shall discover whether the facts in our possession allow us to
point towards a reasonable solution.

Antiquity held, in fact, an almost unanimous opinion in the
matter. This was based on the account given by the first great
Greek historian, Herodotus, of the adventures that brought the
Tyrrhenians to the soil of Tuscany. It is as follows:

In the reign of Atys, son of Manes, a great famine is said
to have occurred in the whole of Lydia. For some time, the
Lydians persisted in carrying on their usual life; then as the
famine did not abate, they sought remedies and some
thought of one thing and some of another. It is said that it
was then that the game of dice, the game of knuckles, games
of ball and other games were invented but not the game
of draughts, the invention of which the Lydians do not
claim. And this is how they made their inventions serve
them in combatting hunger. On any two days they played
throughout one whole day, so as to distract their attention
from the search for food. The next day they stopped playing
and ate. They lived in this manner for eighteen years.

But as the evil, instead of subsiding, continued to grow in violence, the king divided the Lydian people into two groups; and he drew lots for one of them to stay, the other to leave the country. He put himself at the head of the group which was to stay, and at the head of the group which was leaving, he put his son Tyrrhenos. Those Lydians who were designated by lot to leave the country went down to Smyrna, built ships, loaded these ships with all the valuable objects they possessed, and set sail to seek a territory and means of livelihood until, after skirting the shores of many lands, they reached the land of the Umbrians. There they founded towns, in which they live until this day. But they changed their name of Lydians for another, derived from that of the son of the king who had led them. Taking his name as theirs, they called themselves Tyrrhenians.

We do know, in fact, that the Etruscans, whom the Romans called Tusci or Etrusci (hence their present name), were called Tyrrhenoi by the Greeks. From that there derives, in turn, the name of the Tyrrhenian sea on whose shores they built some of their towns. Herodotus thus gives a picture of the migration of an oriental people. The Etruscans are presumed to be none other than Lydians who, according to the chronology of the Greek historians, left their country at a rather late date in the 13th century B.C. and installed themselves on the coast of Italy.

Thus, the whole of Etruscan civilisation would derive directly from the plateau of Asia Minor. Herodotus was writing towards the middle of the 5th century B.C. Taking their cue from him, nearly all the Greek and Roman historians adopted his point of view. Virgil, Ovid and Horace often call the Etruscans Lydians in their poems. According to Tacitus (Annals, IV, 55), under the Roman Empire the Lydian town of Sardes had preserved the memory of this remote Etruscan origin; the Lydians still considered themselves to be brothers of the Etruscans. Seneca takes as an example of the migration of an entire people that of the Etruscans and writes: 'Tuscos Asia sibi vindicat.' Asia claims to have fathered the Tuscans.

Classical writers, then, did not seem to doubt the correctness of the ancient tradition of which, as far as we are concerned, Herodotus is the first exponent. However, a Greek theoretician, Dionysius of Halicarnassus, who lived in Rome under Augustus, considered that he could not adhere to this view. In the first of his works on Roman history he wrote as follows: 'I do not think that the Tyrrhenians were emigrants from Lydia. In fact they do not have the same language as the Lydians; and they cannot be said to preserve any other trait which might be considered to derive from their supposed homeland. They do not worship the same gods as the Lydians; they do not have the same laws and, from this point of view at least, they differ even more from the Lydians than from the Pelasgians. It thus seems to me that those who say that the Etruscans are not a people who came from abroad, but are an indigenous race, are right; to me this seems to follow from the fact that they are a very ancient people which does not resemble any other either in its language or in its customs.'

Thus, since ancient times, two opposing views have been held on the origin of the Etruscans. In modern times the quarrel has flared up again and certain scholars, following Nicolas Fréret who, towards the end of the 18th century, was permanent secretary of the Académie des inscriptions et belles lettres, have seen fit to add a third solution to the two previously proposed. According to them the Etruscans, like the other Italic peoples, came from the North; they were Indo-European invaders and formed part of the successive waves that had broken in turn on the peninsula from 2000 B.C. on. At present this thesis, although it has not been completely abandoned, has very few adherents. Nor does it stand up to the evidence of the facts. We must therefore dispose of it at once in order not to complicate the problem unnecessarily.

The point of departure of this Nordic hypothesis is the apparent connection between the name of the Raeti, the Raetians, an Alpine tribe against whom Drusus, son of Augustus, fought, and the name of Rasena by which, according to the testimony of classical writers, the Etruscans described themselves. The incidence of the Raetians is said to constitute historical proof that in ancient times the Etruscans came down from the North and crossed the Alps. This opinion seems to find confirmation in a passage from Livy which states: 'Even the Alpine populations have the same origin as the Etruscans, particularly the Raetians. The latter have been rendered savage by the very nature of the region, so much so that they have preserved nothing of their ancient fatherland except the accent, and even that in a very corrupt form.' (V, 33 11). Finally, inscriptions in a language similar to Etruscan have in fact been discovered in the regions occupied by the Raetians.

What actually happened here was that correct facts were used to arrive at wrong conclusions. The presence of Etruscans in Raetia is certain. But it does not date back very far, nor to a hypothetical passage of the Etruscans through the alpine valleys. It was only in the 4th century B.C., when the Celtic invasion compelled the Etruscans of the Po plain to flee, that the latter sought refuge in the safe retreats offered by the Alpine foothills. Livy himself, if we analyse his text closely, meant to say no more, and the Etruscoid inscriptions of Raetia, which are all of a late date and not earlier than the 3rd century B.C., can be perfectly well explained by this movement of Etruscan refugees towards the north.

The thesis of an oriental origin has much more validity. Many linguistic and archaeological facts seem to confirm it clearly. This explains why it has remained in great favour with scholars. Many characteristics of Etruscan civilisation recall very closely what we know of the civilisations of ancient Asia Minor. Though various Asiatic aspects of Etruscan religion or art could in the last analysis be explained by chance the partisans of the thesis consider that the Oriental charac, teristics of Etruscan civilisation are too numerous and too imposing; the hypothesis of mere coincidence must, they argue, be excluded.

The national name of the Etruscans, Rasena, is found in various very similar forms in different dialects of Asia Minor. The hellenised name of Tyrrhenoi, or Tyrsenoi, also appears to have its origin on the Anatolian plateau. This term has an adjectival form and appears to be derived from a word Tyrrha or Tyrra. Now, we know of a locality in Lydia which is called precisely Tyrra. We are obviously tempted to relate the Etruscan and Lydian words and to attribute some importance to this curious parallel. To judge by the Latin *turris*, a tower, no doubt derived from this root, Tyrrhenoi would mean liter, ally the men of the citadel, of the high town. The root *tarch* is of great importance in Etruscan. We have only to recall Tarchon, brother or son of Tyrrhenos, founder of Tarquinia and of the dodecapolis—the league of the twelve Etruscan cities. Or, again, the name of the sacred city of ancient Tus, cany, Tarquinia itself. Now, names derived from a root *tarch* —are also numerous in Asia Minor. There they are given to gods or princes.

In 1885, two young scholars of the French School in Athens, Cousin and Durrback, made a major discovery in an island of the Aegean sea, the island of Lemnos. They brought to light, near the village of Kaminia, a decorated and inscribed funerary stele. We see on it in profile the face of a warrior armed with a lance, and two engraved texts, one around his head, the other on one of the lateral faces of the stele. This monument, the product of local archaic art, must date from the 7th century B.C., a period much earlier than the conquest

Fig. 5

of the island by the Greeks in 510. The inscriptions are in the Greek alphabet, but the language used is not Greek. Very quickly the points of contact between this language and Etruscan were noticed. Here and there the inflexions are the same; the formations of the words seem to follow the same rules. It is thus an Etruscoid language, spoken in the island of Lemnos in the 7th century B.C. The stele did not remain an isolated document. Had this been the case its inscription might have been thought the work of an isolated individual— perhaps an Etruscan immigrant. But, shortly before the last war, the Italian school found other fragments of inscriptions in the island, written in the same language. This is none other than the language of the island's inhabitants before its conquest by Themistocles.

Now, if the Tyrrhenians came from Anatolia, they could very well have put in at Aegean islands such as Lemnos, and left small groups. The Kaminia stele, which is more or less contemporary with the birth of Etruscan civilisation in Tus-cany, is easily explicable within the framework of the Oriental hypothesis.

Recourse has been had to anthropology in an attempt to resolve the problem. The systematic study of some forty skulls, discovered in Etruscan tombs by the Italian anthropologist Sergi, has not produced convincing results nor demonstrated a real difference between data from Etruria and from other regions of Italy. Sir Gavin de Beer has recently had the idea of using the genetic evidence of blood groups. The proportion in which the four blood groups are found is more or less constant in each race. A study of them might, therefore, be an indication of the origin and degree of affinity between peoples who are not too widely separated in time. Since the Tuscans enjoyed relative stability in the course of history, they must preserve genes inherited from the Etruscans. Now, the maps of the distribution of blood groups in modern Italy

Fig 5. Funerary stele from Kaminia in the island of Lemnos. National Museum, Athens

give an area in the centre of the peninsula which shows certain differences from the rest of the population and certain affinities with the Eastern peoples. The results of these researches will allow us to assess at its true value this possible indication of Eastern descent. Great prudence must, however, be shown in a field where widely differing factors may account for the same phenomenon.

It would take too long to enumerate all the Etruscan cus-toms, religious beliefs or artistic techniques that have frequently and rightly been linked with the Orient. Let us recall only the salient facts. The position occupied by the woman among the

Plate 38

Etruscans was a privileged one and had nothing in common with the humble and subordinate condition of the Greek woman. This is, however, a mark of civilisation which we also observe in the social structure of Crete and Mycenae. There, as in Etruria, the woman is present at spectacles, per-formances and games and does not—as in Greece—remain cloistered within the quiet halls of the women's quarters. The Etruscan woman takes part in banquets at the side of her husband, and Etruscan frescoes often illustrate her habit of

Fig. 6

reclining beside the master of the house at the banquet table. This custom caused her to be accused, wrongly, of immorality by the Greeks, and later by the Romans. Inscriptions confirm the status of equality seemingly enjoyed by the Etruscan woman; frequently the person dedicating the inscription men-tions, along with the name of his father or even without mentioning it, that of his mother. Now, there is evidence of this use of the matronymic in Anatolia, and particularly in Lydia. Perhaps in it we can see traces of an ancient matriarchy.

In the artistic and religious fields, the points of resemblance increase. Unlike the Greeks and Romans but like many Oriental nations, the Etruscans believed in a revealed religion, whose precepts were jealously preserved in sacred books. Their supreme gods constituted a trinity, worshipped in triple temples. These three deities were Tinia, Uni and Menrva, whom Rome was to worship in its turn under the names of Jupiter, Juno and Minerva. This cult of a trinity, venerated in sanctuaries with three halls, each dedicated to one of the three gods, is also found in the Creto-Mycenaean civilisation. The Etruscan tombs are frequently surmounted by *cippi*, low pillars, either decorated or plain, which is a sign of their presence. These pillars are in local stone; either in *nenfro*, or in volcanic stone, idiorite or basalt. This reminds us of the betylic cult of Asia Minor, where the deity is so frequently represented in the shape of a stone or a column. The egg-shaped pillars of

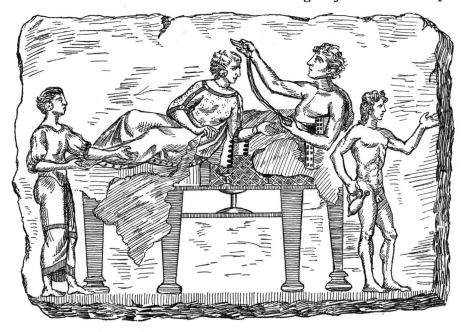

Fig. 6. A couple at a funerary banquet. After an engraving by Byres in Hypogea of Tarquinia, *part IV. pl. 8*

Etruria also represent—in a schematic and symbolic fashion—the dead man as a hero to be worshipped.

Even the ancient world was struck by the Etruscans' uneasy and preoccupied attitude towards the deity, and their constant efforts to attempt to penetrate the future by means of the analysis of omens sent to men by the gods. This religious unease, this constant interest in divination, inevitably brings to mind the similar attitude on the part of many Eastern peoples We shall discuss later at greater length the techniques of divination most favoured by the Etruscans. The Etruscan priests, the *haruspices*, were considered, by the other peoples of antiquity, to be masters in the art of divining. They excelled   Plate 78 in the interpretation of omens and prodigies, and in drawing from these signs the necessary conclusions concerning the conduct of men. Their analytical method always displayed an infinitely complex casuistry. The clap of thunder so closely associated with Tuscan skies, where thunderstorms often burst with frightening and unexpected violence, was the subject of investigations, which astonish us by their detailed and sys-tematic character. The *haruspices* were, in the eyes of the ancients, the uncontested masters of the art of *fulguratura*. Now, certain Oriental peoples, such as the Babylonians, had long before sought to interpret the thunder in order to deduce from it the will of the gods. Babylonian texts have come down to us where the significance of thunder is indicated according to the day of the year on which it occurs. They show a definite kinship with an Etruscan text, which has been preserved in the Greek translation of John Lydus and which is nothing short of an almanac of thunderstorms.

The inspection of the liver and entrails of the victims sacri-ficed to the gods was the favourite activity of the *haruspices*, who appear to have derived their name from it. Etruscan reliefs and mirrors show us these priests engaged in this strange operation, which also reminds us of the ancient Assyro-Babylonian practices. That is not to deny that this technique of divining was known and applied in other countries. There is good evidence of it in Greece, for example. But nowhere else did it assume the overriding importance that it possessed in certain countries of the ancient East and in Tuscany. In Asia Minor and in Babylonia, modern excavations have led to the discovery of a great number of terra-cotta models of livers. On them are engraved prophecies based on the con-figuration of the organs thus represented. Now, similar objects have been found on Etruscan soil. The most famous is the bronze liver discovered in the neighbourhood of Piacenza in 1877. It is divided, on its convex side, into a number of compartments, bearing the names of the Tuscan divinities. Just as these deities occupy very definite regions of the sky, so they hold sway over clearly defined sectors of the victim's liver. The divine origin of the omen depends on the point where the sign is found on the liver; similarly, the lightning was sent by the god, who was master of the region of the sky in which it occurred. There is thus in the eyes of the Etruscans, as in those of the Babylonians before them, a curious parallelism between the liver of the dedicated animal and the world as a whole, the former being only a sort of microcosm, reproducing on a tiny scale the organisation of the world itself.

In the field of art, too, the shapes of certain objects, certain ways of working gold and silver, seem to point to links with the Orient. Gold and silver work had reached a very high Plates 65–67, 69 degree of refinement as far back as the 7th century B.C. The jewels of the Regolini-Galassi tomb are of a perfection and a technical daring that are extremely rare. As we admire them, our minds turn to the subtle techniques used by the gold- and silversmiths of various areas of the Near East.

It is understandable that this converging series of well-established facts should have reinforced the conviction of those who support the Oriental hypothesis. And yet a certain number of scholars of great reputation incline towards the thesis of autochthony, put forward, nearly two thousand years ago, by Dionysius of Halicarnassus. They in no way deny the kinship which links Etruria and the Orient; but they explain it differently. Before the Indo-European invasions, the Mediterranean regions were occupied by ancient peoples bound by complex ties of kinship. The invaders who had come from the north between 200 and 100 B.C., overran nearly all these tribes. But there must have remained, here and there, some elements which survived the general cataclysm. The Etruscans, they say, are precisely one of these little islands that withstood the flood of invasions and explain the Mediterranean features of their civilisation. The indisputable kinship of the Etruscan language with certain prehellenic idioms of Asia Minor and the Aegean, such as that revealed to us by the Lemnian stele, would thus be explained. This is the point of view—and it is a very attractive one—put forward by a number of linguists who are pupils of the Italian scholar, Trombetti. Two recent books, by Massimo Pallottino and Franz Altheim, have expounded this thesis in a reasoned and scientific manner. Both stress one essential point of their argument. For them, the problem up till now has been very badly put. We always ask ourselves where the Etruscans came from as if it were quite natural that an entire people should suddenly come to a region which later on was to become its homeland. The Etruscans are known to us only in the Italian peninsula; in fact their entire history unfolds there. Why, then, should we set ourselves the purely academic question of their provenance? The historian should deal rather with the problem of the formation of the Etruscan nation and its civilisation. In order to solve this problem, he is in no way required to postulate an oriental immigration, which cannot be proved and which is, in any event, very improbable. Herodotus's account should be looked upon as the kind of legendary tale presented in such profusion by ancient writers when they deal with the origin of nations. The Etruscans must derive from a mixture of ethnic elements of various origins, and it is out of this mixture that there emerged an *ethnos*, a nation with well-defined characteristics and physical traits. The Etruscans would thus again become what they should never have ceased to be—namely a purely Italic phenomenon. We can then dispense, without regrets, with the hypothesis of an alien migration, the origin of which would in any event have to be treated with caution.

Such is the gist of the new doctrine which, rejecting the half historic, half legendary tradition, links up in a curious way with the first criticisms made of it by Dionysius of Halicarnassus.

Men with names famous in modern Etruscology have thus declared themselves partisans of the autochthony, or at least partial autochthony, of the Etruscan people and strongly oppose the traditional thesis, though this continues to be sup- ported by a considerable body of scholars.

We must admit that it is not in fact easy to decide in favour of one or other of these theses. The attempts at providing evidence made by Altheim and Pallottino, both of whom set out to prove the *italianità* of the Etruscan people, include some observations which are undoubtedly correct and which stand up to inspection, whatever we may think of their thesis as a whole. It is certainly more important to retrace the strictly historical evolution of the Etruscan people on Tuscan soil than to exhaust one's energy in attempts to identify their more remote origins. That this age-old problem should, to some extent, give way to the question of the shaping of the Etruscan people appears justified. In any event, the complexity of the Etruscan people is beyond doubt. It came into being through the fusion of different ethnic elements and we must abandon the naïve idea of a nation suddenly arising, as if by a miracle, on Italian soil. Even if there was a migration and a wave of invaders from the East, they would, in any case, be numerically only rather small groups who mingled with the Italian tribes long resident between the Arno and the Tiber.

The question, then, is to know whether we should cling to the idea of Anatolian seafarers, who arrived in the Medi- terranean and sought on the shores of Italy a place where they could achieve their ambitions and satisfy their needs.

Looked at from this clearly defined point of view, the tradition of an Oriental migration seems to me to retain all its validity. It alone permits an explanation of the birth, at a precise moment in time, of a civilisation which was to a large extent new, and which had many characteristics linking it to the Creto-Mycenaean and Near Eastern world. If the theory of autochthony were to be carried to its logical conclusion it would be difficult to understand the sudden appearance of industrial and artistic activity, as well as of religious beliefs and rites of which there was no previous indication on Tuscan soil. It has been suggested that it might have been simply a sort of awakening of ancient Mediterranean peoples —an awakening provoked by the development of maritime and commercial relations between the Eastern and Western Mediterranean at the beginning of the 7th century B.C. This argument appears insufficient to explain the almost violent nature of the cultural upsurge in an Italy whose civilisation was still in a backward and, in many respects, primitive stage.

Of course, the migration cannot be placed, as Herodotus claimed, between 1500 and 1000 B.C. Italy enters history at a late date. Throughout the entire peninsula, the Bronze Age extends until about 800 B.C. It is only in the 8th century B.C. that we can place two events of great importance for the history of ancient Italy and consequently for the whole of the Western world—the arrival of the first Greek colonisers on the southern coasts of the peninsula and of Sicily about 750 B.C.; and towards 700 B.C. at the very earliest, according to the indisputable evidence of archaeology, the first flowering of Etruscan civilisation in Tuscany.

Thus, in central and southern Italy, two great centres of civilisation develop more or less simultaneously and both contribute to the awakening of the peninsula from its long slumber. There had previously been nothing on its soil comparable to the brilliant civilisations of the Middle East—those of Egypt or of Babylon. The beginning of Etruscan history, together with the arrival of the Hellenes, marks this awakening. As we retrace the varying fortunes of ancient Tuscany, it is this emergence of Italy into the history of mankind that we shall see coming to life before our eyes.

CHAPTER III

The Enigma
of the Etruscan Language

THE QUESTION OF the Etruscan language is a problem which in spite of the repeated efforts made to solve it, still baffles scholars. This continues to astound the general public. The fact is that innumerable attempts over many centuries by the greatest names in linguistics and comparative philology have failed to decipher a language which was spoken in Tuscany up to the beginning of the Christian era and which the Etruscan priests must have used both in Tuscany and in Rome itself down to the end of the Roman Empire, i.e. down to the end of the 5th century A.D. Yet, in other fields, there has been no lack of discoveries which have permitted us to under-stand idioms seemingly even more difficult to tackle than Etruscan. More than a century ago Egyptian hieroglyphics were deciphered; about ten years ago, the Hittite pictographic language; and, quite recently, the language spoken by the Mycenaeans between 2000 and 1000 B.C., which is known as Linear B. In all these cases the difficulties, although extreme, were duly overcome and the solution of the problems has opened up a magnificent field to linguistic and historical research. The wide interest rightly aroused by the deciphering of Mycenaean at once springs to mind; for from it we learn that at Pylos, at Mycenae and in Crete, the language spoken about 1400 B.C. was very close to Homeric Greek. Let us examine the exact nature of the problem of Etruscan —what progress has been made in deciphering it and what obstacles remain in the way of its interpretation.

SOURCES:

Plate 72

The Etruscan linguistic material that has come down to us is far from negligible. The fertile soil of Tuscany has furnished us with about ten thousand inscriptions, engraved or painted on all kinds of manufactured objects or works of art—mirrors, cists, vases, sculptures, paintings or tiles, columns, funerary urns and sarcophagi. These are epigraphic texts, whose great number must not deceive us; actually, they are nearly all limited to a few words. Nine-tenths of the inscriptions are of a funerary nature and these brief epitaphs tell us only the name of the deceased, his parentage and the age at which he died. We can read them with great ease, for the Etruscan alphabet does not present any real difficulty; for centuries, amateurs and scholars have interpreted these obscure texts without trouble. On the other hand, the problems increase when we are faced with the longer inscriptions, which unfortunately are very scarce. In fact only about ten texts consist of more than one line; only two, one engraved on a tile discovered at Capua, and the other on a *cippus* found near Perugia, consist of about a hundred words.

To these must, however, be added a handwritten text of considerable length. Curiously enough it is written on the twelve linen bandages enclosing a mummy of the Graeco-Roman period, discovered in Alexandria and preserved today in the Zagreb Museum. This is nothing more or less than a linen book, which was put to an unexpected use. It contains fifteen hundred words, but because of the repetitions only five hundred differ from one another. Still, this is already a considerable number, and the Zagreb mummy text is one of the foundations of Etruscological research. It has been possible to establish, in a more or less certain manner, that it is a kind of sacred calendar, enumerating religious ceremonies to be carried

A	A	A	a
B	–	–	(b)
ꓶ	)	)	c
ꓷ	–	–	(d)
ꓱ	ꓱ	ꓱ	e
ꓱ	ꓱ	ꓱ	v
I	I	I	z
꘎	꘎	꘎	h
⊗	⊗	⊙	ʘ(= th)
I	I	I	i
ꓘ	ꓘ	–	k
ꓶ	ꓶ	ꓶ	l
ꟿ	ꟿ	m	m
ꓭ	ꓭ	n	n
⊞	–	–	s
O	–	–	(o)
ꓘ	ꓘ	ꓘ	p
M	M	M	ś
Q	Q	–	q
ꟼ	ꟼ	ꟼ	r
ꙅ	ꙅ	ꙅ	s
T	T	T	t
Y	Y	V	u
X	X	–	ś
Φ	Φ	Φ	φ(= ph)
Ψ	Ψ	Ψ	χ(= ch)
–	–	8	f

Fig. 7. Etruscan alphabets—archaic and later versions (second and third columns)—with their Greek model and transcriptions (first and fourth columns)

out in honour of the gods. The text has been divided into a number of paragraphs and the general sense of the different passages is known. But many points remain obscure, and this fundamental text is far from being really understood.

To these direct sources of information on the Etruscan language we must add other information, some of it indirect, but no less valuable. These are the glossaries of Etruscan words furnished by ancient authors, particularly compilers like Hesychius of Alexandria. When Sir Thomas Dempster—whom we have already mentioned as one of the pioneers of Etruscology—composed his great work on Etruria in 1616–19, he was careful to include this precious material which today is still one of the few clearly defined areas of knowledge. Thus we learn that, in Etruscan, *Aisoi* meant the gods; *capys*, a falcon; *falado*, the sky; *lanista* (which passed into Latin, as did *subulo*, a flute player), a gladiator. Let us add to this the names of the months, to be found in a *Liber glossarum* of the 8th century A.D. The name of the month of June, *aclus*, appears in the form of *Acale* in the manuscript of the Zagreb mummy. All this is very valuable but gives us the meaning of a mere thirty words or so.

In the course of the most recent period of research, the known epigraphic material has been augmented thanks to excavations carried out in various parts of Tuscany and to chance discoveries. Even so, nothing in all this is really likely to bring us any nearer the solution we so greatly desire; yet here and there we glean from the inscriptions newly brought to light, valuable information on the history of the Etruscan cities or on various points in Etruscan linguistics. The most important finds were made on the borders of Etruscan territory proper, at Pompeii and in Latium. During the winter of 1942–3, Maiuri, the eminent archaeologist whose name will always be linked with the scientific excavation of Pompeii, Herculaneum and Campania, found in Pompeii under the foundation of the temple of Apollo, a refuse pit containing various objects dating from 550–460 B.C., including fragments of *bucchero* ware with Etruscan graffiti. He at once recognised them as archaic dedicatory formulae with expressions of the type *mini muluvanice—*

'so-and-so dedicated me . . .' About 500 B.C., then, Pompeii counted among its inhabitants people who spoke Etruscan; this fact would appear to be related to a phase during which the Etruscans exercised brief political and commercial control of the city, between two phases of Greek supremacy which fall in the 6th and 5th centuries B.C.

Etruscan hegemony over Latium and Rome itself in the last decades of the 6th century is mentioned in several Graeco-Latin literary sources. Certain people have questioned it—wrongly so, for Etruscan cultural influence in archaic Latium is confirmed by archaeological discoveries and the presence of the Etruscans can be easily deduced from inscriptions found at Satricum and in Rome itself at the foot of the Capitol.

Certain languages initially presented more difficult problems of interpretation than Etruscan. They presented in fact, two unknowns, the script on the one hand, and the meaning of the words on the other. Linear B, which has recently been deciphered, was a case in point. It is true that in fact this script concealed a dialect very close to ancient Greek and thus familiar to the men who were trying to decipher it. In the case of Etruscan there is only one unknown—the language itself. The Etruscan alphabetic system no longer presents any serious difficulty and its close kindship to the Greek alphabet has long been recognised. The last Etruscan symbol to cause difficulty —the symbol + which was wrongly interpreted as a T—was identified in 1936 by Eva Fiesel as a sibilant. It is therefore perfectly easy to read Etruscan inscriptions—even those one does not understand at all.

Etruscan script certainly poses a problem, but it is a historical one. Can the fact that the Etruscans borrowed a certain type of alphabet from the Greek in any way elucidate the difficult question of their origin? The archaic Greek alphabets can be divided into two large groups, known as Western and Eastern alphabets. The first group gives X the value of x, and the ψ

Fig. 7

the value of Ch. This is initially the case with Etruscan, whilst the most ancient of the alphabets to have been found in fairly large numbers on Etruscan soil—the alphabet of Marsiliana d'Albegna, which dates from about 700 B.C.—has a typically Western character. The question remains as to how this alphabet came to be borrowed. Those who support the Eastern origin theory think it was borrowed by the Etruscans when they were still in their native Anatolia—and their argument has considerable force. The alphabet of Marsiliana d'Albegna still includes the three sibilants of Phoenician origin—particularly the one called 'Samech', which, as far as we know, no Western Greek alphabet possesses. The borrowing of the Etruscan script would thus appear to go back to a period prior to the division of the Greek alphabets into western and eastern groups—prior to the beginning of the Hellenic colonisation in Italy. According to this hypothesis, the Etruscans would only have made this borrowing *before* their migration from the East. However, this argument, strong though it may be, is not decisive. For the Greek alphabets of southern Italy which we possess do not go as far back as that of Marsiliana d'Albegna. Older ones may also have contained the 'Samech', which later fell into disuse, as it was also to do in Etruria. We cannot therefore exclude the possibility that the Etruscans borrowed their alphabet from a Greek colony in the south of the Italian peninsula, in particular from Cumaea, whose Chalcidian alphabet presents many analogies with the Etruscan. Neither of the theses can be dismissed and it is not easy to decide for one or the other.

METHODS OF TEXTUAL INTERPRETATION:

We now come to the perplexing and still unsolved problem of the *meaning* of Etruscan, which is easily read even by a student after only a few months of training and practice. There is a cruel lack of bilingual texts of any scope, yet there is no doubt whatsoever that, did one exist, it would enormously advance research, even if it did not allow us to draw definitive conclusions. But the Etruscan Rosetta stone is not yet in our possession, and we can only draw up a balance sheet of the attempts scholars have made with a tenacity not always favoured by fate.

Since the end of the last century we have become aware of the problem from the methodological point of view. One can attempt to discover the hidden meaning of an Etruscan text in two ways: either by the so-called etymological and deductive method, whereby Etruscan is compared with a language to which it is believed to be related and which is already known, or by the so-called combinatory or inductive method; this latter method does not attempt any external comparison and limits itself to studying Etruscan through Etruscan—that is to say, through a comparison between similar terms and formulae used in different texts, attempts are made to identify the meaning of the words and phrases under study. We must admit that the etymological method has, up till now, almost completely failed. All attempts to find points of resemblance between the Etruscan language and any other idiom, have been entirely fruitless. It would require a long chapter merely to recall all the keys to Etruscan allegedly found by amateurs and scholars —keys which, unfortunately for us, have not been the least use in opening a door which remains resolutely closed. Yet everything seems to have been tried. Efforts have been made to explain the Etruscan language through Greek, Latin, Sanskrit, Hebrew, Albanian, Basque, Hungarian and the Anatolian languages, to mention only the most frequently attempted comparisons. We must bow to the evidence. In the present state of our knowledge, Etruscan stands apart from the various known families of languages, and it seems impossible to find a distant cousin—far less a twin. This does not mean that, used carefully and in very limited instances, the etymological method may not serve a useful purpose. Etruscan, in fact, having been spoken in the centre of the peninsula, was not cut off from the neighbouring idioms. Exchanges and loans, which contact between the various civilisations made not only expedient but inevitable, took place between Etruscan, Latin and Umbrian. The analysis of such borrowings may allow us to explain one set of terms through another.

To judge by the repeated failures of the deductive method, it would appear that Etruscan does not form part of the great family of Indo-European languages. The presence in Etruscan of some words related to Indo-European such as *nefts—nepos* (a grandson); *sac—sacni*, which recalls the Latin *sanctus* and the Umbrian *saahta*, and *tur* (to give), which is close to the Greek *doron*, present no difficulty; for these are, in fact, borrowings made by Etruscan from geographically adjacent languages. Several other examples could be quoted which merely prove the weak penetration of Indo-European elements into the Etruscan vocabulary in the course of the centuries. Actually, a different result would indeed have been surprising. But the construction of the Etruscan sentence has nothing Indo-European about it, nor has the system of the verb as a whole. Thus one cannot distinguish the active and the passive. As for the conjugations, they too do not fit into the coherent system of Indo-European conjugations.

Quite apart from the Graeco-Latin glosses, a fairly large number of Etruscan words can be understood. Why is this so, in view of the fact that, as we have established, the etymological method has almost entirely failed? These concrete results have been obtained by analysing and comparing short epigraphic texts. At the same time deductions were drawn from the nature of the objects bearing the texts. Funerary inscriptions, chiefly those coming from the same tomb, have thus, by comparative analysis, given the meaning of the main words denoting kinship—*clan* (son), *sech* (daughter), *nefts* (grandson), *ati* (mother); but the word for father is still unknown. The same inscriptions have revealed without trouble the meaning of the constantly recurring term, *lupuce* (he is dead). Formulae indicating the age of the deceased have given us the meaning of *avils* (years). Thus, gradually, we have established the meaning of a restricted but basic vocabulary, allowing us to understand very exactly such short epitaphs as '*Partunus Vel Velthurus Satlnal-c Ramthas clan avils lupu XXIIX*, meaning: 'Vel Partunu, son of Velthur and of Ramtha Satlnei died at the age of twenty-eight' (*Corpus inscriptionem etruscarum*, 5425).

Difficulties arise and very quickly multiply when the funer-ary inscriptions become longer and contain information about the life and career of the deceased or when the inscriptions concerned are dedications of objects or monuments. The meaning of the majority of words used escapes us, and the combinatory method, even when applied with the greatest subtlety and care, has not yet thrown any light on the true meaning either of the terms used or of the ideas expressed.

But an ingenious discovery has given rise to another supple-mentary technique, known as the bilingual or parallel text method. It emerges, more and more clearly, that there were reciprocal influences, at different periods, between the various peoples of the Italic peninsula: Etruscans, Latins, Osco-Umbrians and Greeks. This points towards the concept of a relative unity and cultural community in ancient Italy. So the still obscure ritual formulae or prayers we discover in Etruscan texts can be compared with Latin and Umbrian rituals which are bound to show fundamental and formal analogies. This method has already been attempted, not without some success, for the exegesis of the large texts of the Capua tile and the Zagreb book. The collation of the ritual rules described in the latter text, of the brief Roman prayers handed down to us by

Cato in his *De Re rustica*, and verses of prayers on the Umbrian tables in Gubbio, have allowed us to elucidate, at least in general terms, certain passages and certain formulae of the Etruscan ritual.

Naturally, the application of this bilingual method also requires the greatest circumspection. For, if it is possible, in certain cases, to establish the desired analogies between Etruscan writings on the one hand and Latin or Umbrian on the other, the danger, of course, is that of establishing a connection between formulae that are not identical or even analogous. Here too, as in the entire field of Etruscan linguistics, research must be carried out with the greatest possible precautions and an ever vigilant critical judgment. Nevertheless, the first results obtained from the new comparative studies, and from the creation of what are to some extent artificial bilingual texts, are encouraging. Since the new method is of recent provenance, we can expect much of its future application.

THE RESULTS ACHIEVED

Work on Etruscan linguistics has increased in recent years; and it is therefore not easy to establish exactly what results can be considered definitive and what others are still subject to revision. We must limit ourselves to a general picture.

It is undoubtedly Etruscan phonetics that are most familiar to us. The transcription into Etruscan of well-known names of Greek mythology—names of heroes and gods—enables us to grasp fully the fundamental phonetic tendencies of the Etruscan language. At an early date vocalisation is more developed than in the more recent periods, and variations in the quality of vowels are frequent. Thus, the same feminine first name occurs in the forms Ramatha, Rametha, Ramutha

and Ramtha. We note cases of vowel harmony, e.g. Klytai-
mestra in Greek corresponds to the form Cluthumustha. In
general, the voiceless consonants tend to be transformed into
aspirates and aspirates into fricatives. *C* is changed into *ch*,
t into *th*, p *into ph* and *f*. At the beginning of the word, the
aspirate or fricative becomes often the simple aspirate *h*. A
characteristic lack is that of the voiced consonants *b*, *d*, *g*,
which were unknown in Etruscan at least in historical times.
The first syllable of the word is strongly stressed and the frequent result is a syncope of the vowels in the unstressed
syllable. This occurs particularly in the later period and produces complex consonant clusters. To the Greek Alexandros
there thus correspond, on Etruscan mirrors, the forms *Alech-
santre, Elchantre*.

In the field of morphology, our knowledge is by no means
negligible. A number of important facts are now clear to us,
thanks to the work of men like Trombetti and his pupils.
The actual structure of the Etruscan language appears to be
very different from that of the Indo-European languages.
Suffixes used in word formation are interchangeable, and
certain grammatical categories are vague. A curious fact is the
superposition of different suffixes to express a given grammatical
function. The very usual first name *Larth* thus has two geni-
tives *Larthal* and *Larthals*, the latter representing the inflexion
of an already inflected form. It is not easy to reconstruct actual
declensions, but we can distinguish two groups by the form
of the genitive which is either in *s* or in *l*. We can identify
certain personal pronouns (thus *mi* and *mini* are forms of the
first person), the demonstrative pronouns and certain particles.
It is annoying that the enigma of the first six numerals engraved
on the faces of two ivory dice in the Cabinet des Médailles
has not yet been solved, though it is hoped that current research
may soon do so. The Etruscan verb continues to pose grave
problems. Many forms derived from verbal roots have a nominal

aspect. The only forms that are clear to us are the third person singular of the perfect in *ꞁce*: e.g., *mulvenice* means he has dedicated, *turce*, he has given.

On the semantic plane, we have just spoken of the decipherꞁing of a certain number of Etruscan words by various methods. In all, about a hundred roots are at present clearly underꞁstood. They permit us to interpret more or less completely the very brief funerary inscriptions in which the same formulae recur. As soon as words with more complicated concepts appear in the eulogies of the dead or on the longer inscriptions —words absent from the brief epitaphs—literal translation becomes impossible. Frequently, we recognise to which semantic sphere this or that word belongs, but we are unable to give its exact translation. Discussion still continues conꞁcerning the three terms which undoubtedly designate the three principal magistracies in the Etruscan cities: *zilath* or *zilch*, *purthne* and *marunuch*; but, in spite of the efforts of the best brains, their exact meaning is still debated.

In the course of the last few years research on the great ritual texts, found on the tile of Santa Maria di Capua and on the linen book of the Zagreb mummy, has been particularly intense. The conclusions, which one must support, are that these are documents defining the sacrifices to be carried out; and that the rites are enumerated in detailed commandments. The matter set out reminds us of the Umbrian rituals of the Gubbio tablets. The Zagreb text specifies the necessary sequence of the ceremonies and is apparently a religious calendar, giving the months and the days on which feasts are celebrated. The Capua ritual has a funerary character and gives us an idea of the nature of the famous books of Acheron, which contained the Etruscan doctrine on death and life after death. Until recently, the seemingly complicated punctuation of Etruscan texts was not really understood. Its definitive interpretation was completed only a short time ago, and it makes possible the better study of such texts, with the result that interpretation becomes less obscure. This has been the case with the Capua tile, whose text, which is badly damaged into the bargain, was more or less indecipherable before the problem of punctuation was solved. The stops follow consonants at the end of a syllable, as well as the voiced consonants at the beginning of the words. This strange system does not appear in the most ancient inscriptions and is known to us only from the middle of the 6th century. The question of its origin is at present under discussion and it would be too much of a digression to attempt to reproduce here the various interesting hypotheses that have been advanced to account for it. However, the system is now known and Etruscan hermeneutics has greatly profited from it.

PRESENT PROSPECTS

What has been said above shows the point reached in research on the Etruscan language. Methods of approach have undoubtedly been perfected and enriched, and studies are no longer carried on in the dark as was too long the case. At the same time, slow but sure progress has been made in all the sectors of this difficult quest. A grammar of the Etruscan language can, and has been, written. Admittedly it still has a number of obscure points, but it also contains a mass of definite rules that no longer warrant discussion. It is the hermeneutics, that is to say, the translation of the texts, which leaves most to be desired. Our vocabulary is very slender, and this seriously handicaps the most serious attempts to interpret the texts in our possession.

What can we expect from the future? It is difficult to answer such a question, for the reply depends upon an unforeseeable factor—namely, the number and importance of inscriptions which either chance or organised excavations will bring to light. If the material at the disposal of the scholars is not enriched in a decisive manner, progress in Etruscan hermeneutics will very probably be slow and each new conquest will be achieved through a vast number of efforts, few of which will prove successful. It is highly improbable that a comparison with any other known tongue not so far attempted would throw any light on the nature of the Etruscan language. Only the methods defined above will permit an advance, which will be constantly retarded by difficulties and obstacles.

However, it is not unreasonable to hope for a change in the situation through the discovery, either in the East, or in Etruria, of unexpected documents which would shed light on all or part of this still mysterious field. Archaeology, too, now has at its disposal more accurate methods and can draw on a series of techniques of recent date, which greatly facilitate research and discovery. The Anatolian plateau, still so little known, may yield surprises as a result of fresh surveys. Or the Etruscan soil, which excavators continue to examine with a zeal inspired by the increasing number of discoveries, may yet produce a key document—a really extended or, above all, a bilingual text, in Etruscan and in some already known language such as Latin or Greek. Such bilingual documents must in all probability have existed and must have been posted on the walls of Etruscan cities, after their conquest by Rome, during the centuries when the Tuscan population and Roman people co-existed and shared the same life and the same laws. Until recently, excavation has concentrated on tombs, on cemeteries where the scholar is certain, in the event of making a discovery, to come across admirably preserved objects that are often of great artistic value. On the rocky plateaux where the Tuscan cities stood, discoveries are less spectacular and the pick brings to light only the ruined remains of religious or civic buildings. But history and linguistics can expect much from such investigations. The ancient soil of Tarquinii has recently yielded fascinating eulogies, written in Latin, but dealing with the life and careers of Etruscan citizens of a very remote period whom their descendants wished to honour in a dignified manner by laudatory inscriptions. These texts, although comparatively short and very mutilated, have thrown valuable light on the public institutions of the Etruscan cities. We can imagine what benefit the linguist could derive from similar texts, written in two languages. It would mean that at last an age-old enigma could be solved and full light cast on a problem which all the efforts of scholars have hitherto been unable to unravel.

PART THREE

THE HISTORY OF
THE ETRUSCAN PEOPLE

CHAPTER IV

Birth and Expansion

W E CAN PROPERLY UNDERSTAND a people and its history only when we have a knowledge of the region where it came into being and developed, and a clear idea of its state of culture at the moment of its initial expansion. What, then, are the main characteristics of Tuscany and what was its pre-Etruscan past? Only a detailed answer to these two questions will permit us to place the emergence of this new civilisation in space and in time.

Figs. 8, 11, 16

At the zenith of their power the Etruscans were to dominate Italy from the plain of the Po to Campania. But, even then, Tuscany would still have been the vital centre and very heart of their empire. This fine wooded region, rich in colour, extends from north to south between the Arno and the Tiber and is bounded to the east by part of the course of the Tiber itself and by the broken line of the Appenines. It opens broadly on to the Tyrrhenian Sea. One of the essential geographical features of the whole peninsula is the extraordinary way in which it is broken up. The complicated chain of the Appenines produces a division of its territory into distinct regions, separates the east and west seaboards, divides and isolates the fertile plains of the country—those of the Po, of Latium and of Campania. Tuscany, too, has these basic characteristics in an extreme form. The Appenines thrust their lowest slopes into it and the entire region is merely a succession of hills, valleys and mountains, leaving room only for limited plains along the rivers, by the lakes or on the coast. In either case, similar causes have similar effects. Throughout the long peninsula with its self-contained regions, the local characteristics of the various provinces have always been marked. In modern times the unification of the country

Fig. 8

was carried out only with difficulty and at a late date. Simi-larly, the divided nature of Tuscany explains why the different Etruscan cities always preserved a genuine autonomy and merely formed a federated state held together by rather loose bonds.

Italy lacks great rivers; only the Po, in the North, is worthy of that name. However, there are rivers of some importance in Tuscany—the Arno, the Chiani, a tributary of the Arno, and, above all, the Tiber itself. But these rivers are navigable only for part of their course and border the Etruscan territory without penetrating it to any extent. Some rivers cross the country diagonally before flowing into the Tyrrhenian Sea. But these are mere torrents running through the different zones without uniting them. The only genuine connecting link, the coast, extends for 200 miles, and its numerous bays enabled ports to be established, from which expeditions would be launched to near and distant parts. The Etruscans were to take advantage of them to develop their maritime activities and thus acquire, in the eyes of the ancient world, a well-merited reputation as daring sailors and redoubtable pirates.

Such a mountainous region could not be favourable to agriculture. On the other hand, it permitted the breeding of cattle and other flocks. The forests, which in antiquity were denser than they are today, furnished the hunter with abundant game whilst on the sea and on the lakes—which are large and numerous throughout the length of the country—fishermen constantly and successfully plied their skill. Hunting and fishing were to be the favourite sports of the rich Etruscans; furthermore, they confidently expected to rediscover in the other world the pleasures they had so greatly prized on earth. Thus we find in their tombs, the arms and implements which they had used on land and sea, and some of the frescoes recall their exploits.

But the chief wealth of Tuscany lay in its vast mineral deposits which in prehistoric times undoubtedly attracted

Fig. 8. Principal Etruscan sites in Tuscany and Latium

navigators in search of a place to settle. The Etruscans exploited them intensively throughout their history. From the
north of the country to the neighbourhood of Siena, the hills,
known today as the Colline Metallifere (Metalliferous Hills),
contain iron, copper, zinc and tin in large quantities. The
extraction and the working of these metals were at the root of
the wealth and power of the Etruscan nation. The island of

Elba, situated very close to their coasts and for long an integral part of their Empire, offered the same possibilities and was the scene of similar activities.

What stage of culture and general evolution had Tuscany reached between 2000 and 1000 B.C. when the Etruscans appeared? There is evidence of a Bronze Age civilisation there as in the rest of Italy, but it had not been particularly brilliant. About 1000 B.C., new waves of invaders swept across the peninsula, bringing with them techniques for working iron and using them to reduce the earlier populations to slavery. During this first Iron Age, the most important inhabited centres were partly north of the Appenines in the Po plain, and partly in a vast area corresponding to Latium, present-day Tuscany and Umbria. In both cases there developed an extremely active civilisation which is conveniently called 'Villanovan', after Villanova, a hamlet near Bologna, where excavations first revealed its existence.

Figs. 4, 9, 10

This Villanovan civilisation is clearly distinguished by certain characteristic features. Few remains of Villanovan villages and installations survive today. On the other hand, the documentation provided by tombs is ample. Generally, at least up to about 750 B.C., the Villanovans cremated their dead and deposited their ashes in ossuaries which are usually biconical. This shape already appears prior to 1000 B.C. in the pottery of the Bronze Age. Now it becomes universally adopted and found everywhere. The ossuary is made of rather crude pottery, which the Italians call *impasto*, a kind of impure, badly fired clay. It has one handle, or two, and is covered, when in the tomb, by a small cup turned upside down. Some-

Plate 28

times this cup is replaced by a helmet with a great crest of laminated bronze. The significance of this rite can be under-stood at once. The cup or helmet represents in a schematic and crude manner, the head of the deceased. This is the very modest beginning of funerary sculpture which, as we shall

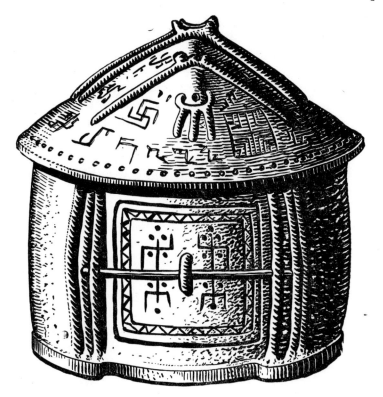

Fig. 9. Terra-cotta hut urn from the Alban Hills. Engraved geometrical decoration

see, flourished later in the Etruscan cemeteries. In Latium, however, and particularly in the area of Albano, the ashes of the dead were placed not in a biconical urn but in one shaped like a shepherd's hut. Hence the name 'hut' urn. Many such objects have been found in Rome itself—in particular in the vast cemetery excavated at the beginning of the century in the Forum by the Italian archaeologist, Boni.

The hut urn was clearly made on the model of the dwellings of the living. In these humble shapes we find the very image

Fig. 9

87

of the huts that must have sheltered the first occupants of Roman soil on the summit of the seven hills—those Latin or Sabine shepherds round whom tradition has cast a legendary halo. Yet the first subjects of Romulus and Remus must have led the simple life of primitive shepherds and cowherds. By revealing the remains on the Villanovan sites, archaeology has allowed us to form a clearer picture of the early stages of the occupation of the Roman hills. There is nothing more instructive than this illumination of legend by history.

Biconical ossuaries or hut urns were laid in a kind of pit dug out of the rock or sometimes in the ground. Inside these funerary vessels—or else, beside them—were placed a whole series of offerings. For men, it was their weapons—bronze or iron-tipped lances, bronze helmets, iron daggers or swords.

Fig. 4 For women, there were their *fibulae*, those bronze clasps and safety pins which held together the material of their dresses. These *fibulae* are extremely valuable for us because their forms alter according to the different periods and, thanks to them, we can date all the material uncovered. The women's tombs also contained a wide range of objects—plaques and jewels of amber and bronze, combs, needles, spindles and everything the deceased had used in their daily tasks. Right from this primitive period, the funerary cult reflects a preoccupation constantly to reappear in ancient Italy; it is aimed at furnishing the deceased with everything he used in life, for he would need it again after his death. For the men of antiquity death was not a total eclipse; those who had died continued to lead in the tomb a life which had, admittedly, a slower rhythm but still retained the characteristics of life on earth. Therefore they had urgent need of offerings and sacrifices. In antiquity neglect of the careful ritual owed to the dead was always considered an unpardonable crime.

For long, the decoration of the Villanovan artifacts in ceramic or bronze remains very simple. It is purely geometric in inspiration and consists of straight or broken lines, zigzags, triangles and swastikas. Then these decorative elements, whether engraved or painted, become richer and more complicated. Towards the middle of the 8th century B.C., we are conscious of a transformation in customs and rites. The deceased is no longer invariably incinerated; the rite of inhuma-

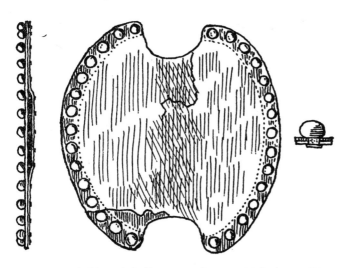

Fig. 10. Bronze buckler with double groove, perhaps intended for dancing. Discovered in 1955 near Bolsena. 700 B.C. Breadth 12 in.

tion appears and gains ground. In addition to the well tomb, we now find the ditch tomb, marked at its four corners by stones or gravel. Bronze objects increase in numbers. Vases of laminated bronze, which preserve the ancient biconical shape, become notable for their elegance and the originality of their engravings. Flattened bronze flasks, helmets, blunt or pointed, and round bronze bucklers recall objects and shapes frequently found in the Aegean civilisation of the Eastern Mediterranean. The human figure, presented in a very schematic

Fig. 10

89

manner, is introduced as a decorative element. In all this we feel foreign influences. From 750 B.C. onwards, Greek navi-gators begin to settle on the southern coasts of Italy and Sicily. They must have had contact with the inhabitants of the Tuscan coasts.

At the end of the century, the modifications in the shape of objects and in the architectural structure of the tombs become more pronounced. In the north of Etruria, at Vetulonia and Populonia, monumental mausoleums appear, very different from the humble tombs of the preceding period. They are great tumuli, made of earth and stones, with the tomb built inside. This takes the shape of an actual chamber, surmounted by a vault or dome, which is formed by the superimposition of stone blocks, laid flat and regularly overlapping. These false vaults and false domes are merely the forerunners of the classical forms of Etruscan and Roman architecture. Monu-ments of this type are directly linked with buildings found in Asia Minor and in the Aegean basin between 2000 and 1000 B.C. They recall in a strange way the famous tombs of Mycenae. The date when they appear coincides in Tuscany with the beginning of a new type of civilisation whose oriental characteristics are obvious. It is usually described as 'orient-alising'. This period marks the exact beginning of Etruscan history proper. And whether or not we accept in all its aspects the traditional idea of a migration of seafarers from the Eastern Mediterranean, it is something essentially oriental that now appears on Italian soil.

THE BEGINNINGS OF ETRUSCAN POWER.
THE ETRUSCANS AND THE SEA

From the beginning of its existence the Etruscan people appeared in the eyes of the ancient world to be a rich and powerful nation, and we have the same impression today when we see the sumptuous objects which in the 7th and 6th century tombs had been reverently placed beside the dead. The *fibulae*, necklaces, bracelets and archaic ear-rings reveal goldsmith's art of extreme beauty.

All these exquisitely worked jewels are the tangible remains of the splendour which Etruria knew from the beginnings of its history. This period coincides with the great period of Greek colonisation in the West. Eastern influences, at first Phoenician and Cypriot, and, from the end of the 7th century onwards, mainly Greek, appear in the scenes that decorate the goblets or the silver-gilt vessels. Here themes borrowed in turn from the Egyptian, Mesopotamian or Syrian repertoire form a complicated mixture. As in all Mediterranean art of this period, fantastic animals—chimerae, sphinxes and winged horses—occupy an important place. This contributes to the aura of mystery surrounding the products of the Etruscan workshops. With these creations of local origin are intermingled numerous objects imported from abroad—from Sardinia, Egypt or Syria.

Plates 69, 70

Plate 36

The abundant riches of these tombs, which have rightly been called 'tombs of gold', show that Etruscan prosperity had developed with surprising speed. The copper and iron mines around Populonia must already have been exploited. The nation drew from them a vast purchasing power enabling it to import on a large scale the gold, silver and ivory needed by the workshops of its craftsmen and artists.

To safeguard this trade they required sea power sufficient to meet any challenge. And in fact the Etruscans enjoyed a supremacy which inspired respect in the western seas. It was a period when a great movement drew the industrious peoples of the Eastern world—the Phoenicians and the Greeks— towards the distant and still savage countries of the West, in search of trading posts, markets and wealth. The mineral

Fig. 11

deposits of Spain, Sardinia and Italy were a rich bait. It was then that powerful states were born—in Africa, in Spain and on the coasts of Sicily and Italy. Greeks and Phoenicians established solid bases destined to have a glorious and adventurous future. In this vast arena there began a bitter struggle for the conquest of raw materials, a struggle which already foreshadowed the clash of the great modern empires. For centuries Greeks and Phoenicians were to meet as rivals, and this clash preceded the decisive duel for world power between Rome and Carthage.

It was in this turbulent world of pioneers and adventurers that the great Etruscan adventure began. We lack many such details as would cast more light on this remote period. Both texts and archaeology, however, leave no doubt as to Etruscan maritime power. Facing them were the sailors of Greece and Carthage. Greek texts abound in allusions to Etruscan naval strength. They describe it, perhaps because of natural rancour against old enemies, as a pirate force manned by terrible corsairs. The Homeric hymn to Dionysius recalls the daring abduction of the God by Tyrrhenian pirates whom his magic powers transform into dolphins. Plutarch relates the rape by the Etruscans of the women of Brauron, in Attica. They dared to carry off the statue of Hera from Samos. And their bold raids on the Greek coasts of Italy and Sicily were without number.

But we must take into account the ill-feeling of the Greeks against their rivals, if we wish to assess correctly the naval policy of young Etruria. They first turned their attention to the island of Elba, a great iron-producing centre, and their sailors were quickly able to occupy it. The larger islands of Corsica and Sardinia offered numerous safe harbourages for ships bound for distant lands. Sardinia was the seat of an ancient civilisation, famed for its cyclopean constructions, the *nuraghi*, and for its strange small, spindly bronzes, which are curiously

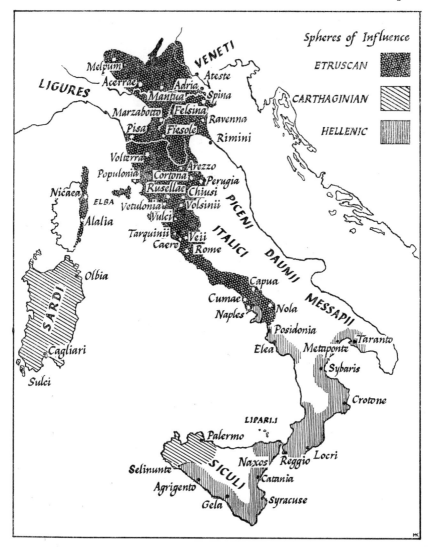

Fig. 11. Italy at the peak of Etruscan power

modern. Commercial relations between Etruscans and Sardinians began very early, as is proved by objects of Sardinian manufacture discovered in the necropoleis of Vetulonia. Both peoples possessed skilful craftsmen in bronze and developed their metallurgical activities along parallel lines. As for Corsica, it was to be the stake in a bitter struggle between Etruscans and Greeks.

Etruscan seamen and merchants traded or plundered in regions which even today show traces of their passage—the coasts of Provence and Spain, from Marseilles to Catalonia, the African coast and the shores of Greece. This rapid maritime expansion led to complete domination of the Tyrrhenian Sea by the Etruscans, to what the Greeks called the Etruscan *thalassocracy*. This achievement must have been the work of the great coastal cities, Caere, Tarquinii, Vulci, and further north, Vetulonia and Populonia.

But the Tuscan navy encountered two powerful adversaries barring its way. An increasing number of Greeks were settling on the coasts of Campania and Sicily, brought there by that vast colonising movement which was to have such an influence on the future of the West. The Phoenicians of Carthage, for their part, were extending their sphere of influence in western Sicily and, nearer to Tuscany, on the western and southern shores of Sardinia, where they founded such cities as Cagliari, Sulci and Nora. The three great maritime powers of the Western Mediterranean had too many ambitions in common to be able to continue their expansion without clashing. In the 6th century hostilities and alliances took shape.

It was in fact then that the Greek colonisers from the coast of Asia Minor, avoiding the over-populated regions of Sicily and southern Italy, spread along the eastern coast of Spain and the coast of Provence where they founded Antibes, Nice and, above all, Marseilles. The Etruscans now felt threatened by the Greeks both in the North and in the South and wished

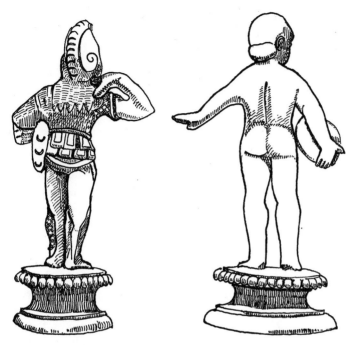

Fig. 12. Small bronzes serving as end-figures to candelabra: a warrior and a discus-thrower

to free themselves from this pincer movement, which must have become even more intolerable when, in the middle of the 6th century, the Greeks setting out from their new posses-sions on the Ligurian coast, founded Alalia on the eastern shore of Corsica and perhaps also Olbia in the north of Sardinia. This coincides with the arrival in these regions of Phocaean refugees fleeing from Persian domination in Asia Minor.

Etruria decided to face its dangerous enemy. It accepted the Carthaginian penetration of Sardinia as a *fait accompli*, although fundamentally it cannot have liked it, and concluded with Carthage a treaty of alliance which was subsequently several times renewed. Its clauses were of great importance; they envisaged trade, mutual respect of conquests, and a military alliance. Corsica remained in the Etruscan sphere; Sardinia, under Carthaginian influence. Aristotle in his *Politics*, recalls this formidable alliance against Hellenism. The clash was not long in coming. About 540 B.C., Greek ships engaged the allied Carthaginian and Etruscan fleets. According to the account given by Herodotus, the Greeks compelled their enemies to retreat. But, in reality, they must have been defeated, for they were subsequently forced to evacuate Corsica, a territory rapidly occupied by the Etruscans, who founded a new town there which they called 'Victory'. The Etruscan fleet thus maintained the upper hand in the northern Tyrr-henian. But the great victor in the struggle was certainly Carthage. She effectively protected her lines of communica-tions, which brought her the silver of Spain and the tin of Great Britain. She had a firm hold on that vital point—the Straits of Gibraltar. And she soon came to consider the seas between Sardinia, Africa and Spain as her exclusive property. Whilst the bitter duel between Carthage and Greece for the possession of Sicily continued, Etruria lost the possibility of extending her seaways and, in the restricted zone allotted to her, she would find it difficult to preserve her status in face of the renewed assaults of the Greek navies. In the 5th century the Etruscan thalassocracy crumbled and Etruria's continental possessions were also seriously threatened. Thus the 7th and 6th centuries B.C. were the period of Etruria's ephemeral supremacy over the Italian peninsula.

CHAPTER V

The Continental Hegemony of Etruria. Its Decline and the Roman Conquest

UNLIKE THE GREEKS in Italy, who limited their positions on the mainland to coastal towns and their surrounding territories, the Etruscans penetrated deep into Italy. Tuscany no longer satisfied their ambitions. During the 6th century B.C. they therefore occupied a considerable part of the Po valley in the north, and in the south Latium and the rich plain of Campania. These pirates of the Western seas founded a vast empire on land and came near to unifying the whole of Italy. In Roman times people remembered this period of Etruscan hegemony and Livy recalls these glorious pages of her history.

Etruscan penetration might have gone eastwards—beyond the Abruzzi, towards the shores of the Ionian sea. But east of the Tiber, an Italic nation offered an obstacle difficult to overcome. The Umbrians were firmly entrenched in the region now called after them, and in that direction the line of the Tiber remained the permanent frontier of the Etruscan people. The vast territories to the north of the Appenines were, on the other hand, occupied only by scattered tribes, ill equipped to oppose the entry of a regular army into the Po valley. Etruscan merchants must earlier have reconnoitred this fertile valley, beyond which they could trade with the Alpine populations and establish contact with the tribes of Germany and Gaul. Their accounts led the Etruscans to cross the chain of the Tusco-Emilian Appenines in force in the second part of the 6th century B.C. and begin the methodical conquest of the country. First they occupied Bologna, in Etruscan *Felsina*, which rapidly grew into a great Etruscan city and was the

Plate 37

centre of the new northern empire. Its importance increased when the Etruscans, having reached the Adriatic, founded trading posts there. After the occupation of Ravenna and Rimini, Spina was founded at one of the mouths of the Po. The wealth of its necropoleis bears witness to its opulence in the 5th century. A large part of the trade with the Adriatic coasts and with Greece itself passed through this new colony. There were certainly about a dozen large Etruscan towns in the Po valley and they must have formed a federation like that of their capital cities in Etruria. It was thanks to their positions and their wealth that relations between Tuscany and the, as yet savage, countries of the north were able to develop. Countless Etruscan bronze and gold objects, dating from that period, have been discovered to the north of the Alps and particularly in Burgundy and Switzerland.

The Etruscan merchants thus became middlemen for Greek works of art which the Celtic tribes beyond the Alps ordered in the cities of Greece or of Magna Graecia, in exchange no doubt for their good offices in regulating the tin trade. Indeed Hellenic penetration of the Celtic world seems, apart from the direct route through Marseilles and up the Rhône, also to have followed an indirect route across the Alpine passes with the Etruscans as go-betweens. Perhaps the Danube route also played a certain part. At all events Graeco-Etruscan influence on Celtic civilization at the end of the Hallstatt and the beginning of the La Tène period is by no means negligible. The hoard recently discovered in the tomb of a princess at Vix, near Dijon, contains a variety of material—Greek, Etruscan and Celtic. The Greek objects—in particular the immense bronze krater, or wine-bowl, which must have been manufactured in a city of Magna Graecia—came into Burgundy thanks to the trade organised by the Etruscan merchants.

Etruscan territorial ambitions were not limited to the north of the peninsula. A similar impulse drew them towards the plains of Latium and Campania; and their power thus asserted itself to the south of Tuscany from the end of the 7th century onwards and throughout the following century. This had a decisive impact on the history of Rome itself, and the fate of the West was thereby profoundly affected.

The Latin peoples formed a confederation of an essentially religious character. Rome, which was as yet only a small town without great political or military importance, was one of the

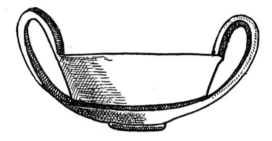

Fig. 13. Bucchero cantharos, *about 600 B.C., from Cerveteri. Villa Giulia Museum Rome*

members of this league. Powerful Etruria was able to maintain her dominion over all the Latin tribes without difficulty, and her soldiers established themselves in Rome, whose position was of particular importance to them. Set on moderately high, but steep hills beside the Tiber, about ten miles from its mouth, Rome was an easily defended strongpoint. It was of primary importance for the Etruscans to hold this advantageous site firmly.

Tradition has preserved a clear memory of the Etruscans in Rome; the Tuscan dynasty of the Tarquins is said to have held sway from 616 to 510 B.C. Archaeological discoveries confirm the accuracy of this tradition. The story as told by ancient authors is as follows. In the reign of Ancus Martius, a Latin king, a rich inhabitant of the Etruscan town of Tarquinii, Lucumon by name, settled in Rome. Lucumon's wife was a

high-born Etruscan named Tanaquil. The couple's arrival in
Rome was marked by a significant omen. On the Janiculum
an eagle swooped down and snatched off Lucumon's hat.
Then it circled round the chariot of the two newcomers,
uttering piercing cries, before replacing the headgear on the
head of its owner who was overcome with amazement.
Tanaquil received this divine omen with joy. To her it indicated clearly that the gods placed the highest hopes in her
husband. Lucumon settled in Rome and took the name of
Lucius Tarquinius Priscus, Tarquin the Elder. Thanks to his
savoir faire and his persuasive oratory, he succeeded in having
himself elected King on the death of Ancus Martius.

In this astonishing tale, we find certain characteristic traits
of Etruscan divinatory methods. Let us look more closely at
the reaction of Tanaquil who, according to Livy, was versed
in the science of divine omens. According to her, all the
evidence encouraged Lucumon to cherish the highest hopes:
the very nature of the bird which had providentially intervened;
the region of the sky from which it had descended; the identity
of the god whose messenger it was—Jupiter, the king of the
gods as the eagle is the king of the birds; finally, the part of
the body—namely the head, the most noble part of man. We
should note the importance accorded here—in keeping with
the Etruscan method of interpreting omens—to the direction
from which the omen came and the interplay established
between purely material factors and the moral significance with
which they are endowed. The flames which, when he was a
child, surrounded the head of Servius Tullius, foretelling his
accession to the throne after the death of Tarquin the Elder,
and the completely preserved human head discovered when
the Etruscan tyrants were building the temple of Capitoline
Jove, were prodigies of the same nature and presaged the
greatness of the man and of the sanctuary. Six centuries later,
a similar miracle announced the future greatness of Octavius,

Fig. 14. Bucchero cantharos, *with engraved drawings; 7th century B.C. Villa Giulia Museum, Rome*

the emperor to be. An eagle, Suetonius tells us, swooped down and seized the bread he was holding in his hand, then gently restored it to him.

Thus the Etruscans, from their first appearance on Roman soil, brought with them the concepts and divinatory techniques cherished in the region from which they had come. In fact, it was Etruscan civilisation in its entirety that established itself on the seven hills. The name of Lucumon, which Livy regards as the name of the king, is, in fact, not that of an individual. To the Etruscans it meant the supreme head, the lord. Each town in the Etruscan federation had its *lucumon*. We note too the naïveté of the account, when Lucumon changes his name to Lucius Tarquinius Priscus, i.e. Tarquin the Elder. The cognomen Priscus, must have been ascribed to him at a later date, to distinguish him from his son and successor.

Tarquin the Elder is said to have been the son of a Greek from Corinth, named Demaratus. This tradition, which we are not in a position to check, recalls, however, the influence exercised upon 6th-century Etruria by the Greek towns, and in particular by the Pelopponesian city of Corinth. Etruscan royalty is represented in Roman tradition by only three persons —Tarquin the Elder and his son Tarquin the Proud, between whom there comes Servius Tullius, a man without ancestry. But the last-named also bore himself like a great Tuscan monarch. The emperor Claudius, in the speech he delivered in A.D. 48, which was recorded on a bronze tablet not long since discovered at Lyons, tells us that in Etruscan Servius Tullius was called Mastarna. Now, the frescoes of the François tomb at Vulci show two brothers, Aulus and Caelius Vibenna fighting alongside a chief named Mastarna, against another warrior whom the inscription calls the Roman Cnaeus Tarquin. Thus the Etruscan version of the legend shows us the three Etruscan kings of Rome as *condottieri* whose wars reflect the hostility which set the Etruscan cities against each other. Perhaps the kingship of Servius is proof of a temporary triumph in Rome of the chiefs of the powerful 'Lucumony' of Vulci. A recently discovered *bucchero* vase dating from the period in question, bears the name of Aulus Vibenna and confirms the historicity of the protagonists of the tradition.

Figs. 13, 14, 21, 22

Livy stresses the importance of the political and military measures taken by the Tuscan kings, their conquests of Latin towns, their vast building programmes for civil and religious purposes. Some of the measures attributed by him to this period, seem to be antedated; but the gist of his account is confirmed by the results of excavations carried out in Rome. Rome, before the Etruscans, was rather a collection of villages than a real town. The Etruscans made a city of it, comparable to the royal capitals of southern Etruria. At this date an outer wall of local *tufa* was built round the seven hills to ensure their defence. This outer wall, with its vast perimeter, was rebuilt after the invasions by the Gauls in 378 B.C. The Tarquins installed an effective system of drainage—the *Cloaca Maxima*—

which transformed the swampy plain of the Forum and made it for the first time the meeting place of the Popular Assembly. The imposing foundations still extant on the Capitol, in the basements of the *Museo dei Conservatori*, are the tangible remnants of the famous temple dedicated by the Tarquins to the Capitoline Triad in the last years of the 6th century B.C. In accordance with Etruscan custom, the sanctuary comprised three sacred chambers, three *cellae*, dedicated to Jupiter, Juno and Minerva, who were worshipped there under their Etruscan names. The triple plan of the sanctuary was respected through-out the many reconstructions of the temple in the Roman period. When Rome was establishing innumerable colonies in the provinces of its Empire, a Capitoline sanctuary was built in the centre of these cities—a replica of the venerable edifice which they owed to the science and art of the architects of the Tarquins.

Etruscan kingship introduced into Rome all the external signs and emblems which, in the Tuscan cities, denoted in the eyes of the people the glory and the power of the *lucumones*. Thus the Tarquins wore the golden crown, the golden ring and the sceptre. Their ceremonial garment was the *toga palmata*, and the lictors who opened the processions carried on their shoulders the awe-inspiring *fasces* as a sign of the un-limited power of the Prince. The *fasces* were made of rods for scourging and an axe, which was a ceremonial weapon and a symbol of the political and religious power of the leader. This material symbol of sovereign power was retained by Rome after the departure of the Tarquins and the beginnings of the Republican régime. There was then allotted to the consuls, who exercised power for one year only, supreme power over the legions—a step that removed the danger of the return of the Monarchy. Similarly, the triumph which was celebrated after victory over the enemies of Rome repeated, throughout Rome's history, the religious rites enjoined by

Fig. 15. Bronze statu-ette of Minerva in battle; beginning of 5th century B.C. British Museum, London

Etruscan royalty when its adversaries had been routed. During this solemn procession which ended at the Capitol with a sacrifice to Jupiter, the commander, standing in his war chariot and directing his cortège of prisoners and soldiers, identified himself temporarily with the supreme deity.

The hold of the Etruscans over Latium enabled them to turn covetous eyes on the rich lands of Campania. This fertile and hospitable country offered great possibilities for agricultural exploitation. The native tribes—the Ausones and Opici—who were related ethnically and by custom to the Latins, were comparatively small in number and could not put up a very serious resistance to the invaders. The Greeks, who were firmly installed on the coasts, did not penetrate into the hinterland. Thus, here, the Etruscan conquest was literally an occupation of the land. This was shared out among the new colonisers in accordance with ancient principles of land division, in the form of allotments, marked off into skilfully and regularly defined squares. The Etruscans had, in fact, an extensive knowledge of surveying and mensuration, and the Roman surveyors, some of whose writings have come to us, in their turn learnt to apply the principles that lay behind this ancient technique. The division of Italy and the Roman provinces into squares with sides of 710 m.—which, in various areas and in particular in North Africa, is revealed to us by aerial photography and astonishes by its extraordinary extent and perfect geometry, thus goes back to the Tuscan heritage. In Campania, the Etruscans founded numerous towns which formed a prosperous federation, linked closely to the mother country. The chief amongst them was Capua, which was also built according to the usual norms, in the centre of a region divided up like a chessboard. The Volturno river put it in direct communication with the coast, and this favoured the development of its commercial relations. Nola, Acerra, Nocerra, were other important and prosperous centres.

An expansion of this nature in the hinterland of Campania was obviously a new source of conflicts with the Greeks. We can imagine the danger constituted by the presence of their hereditary enemy in their rear. For the numerous Hellenic trading posts along the coast and even for the powerful city of Cumae, whose foundation goes back to the 8th century B.C., their proximity constituted a constant menace. Hostilities between the two opponents inevitably broke out. The Etruscans attempted to instal themselves on the coast and to deal finally with Cumae, their most powerful rival. But their efforts, which might well have been decisive, were unsuccessful. A great expedition, for which the Etruscans had assembled both their own forces and local contingents recruited from distant Apulia, failed under the very walls of Cumae owing to the stubborn resistance of the Greeks under their energetic leader, Aristodemus. The year 524 marked the collapse of Etruscan hopes for the complete conquest of Campania. The Etruscans emerged further down the coast, however, through the Sarno valley, and for a time they controlled Pompeii, Herculaneum and Sorrento. They also occupied the Gulf of Salerno. The Silaris river was the extreme limit of their southward expansion. Beyond it lay a region held entirely by Greek colonisers. But the empire set up by the Etruscans at the end of the 6th century was already vast, and they may well have thought it would be possible for them to unify the peninsula to their own advantage. But the fortunes of war were to decide matters otherwise; from the 5th century onwards, the structure they had so rapidly built on such a vast scale began to encounter a difficult period. The story of this progressive decline, to the accompaniment of the advance of Rome and its legions, was to last for nearly two hundred and fifty years, until the submission of the whole of Etruria to the Roman eagle.

THE DIFFICULTIES OF ETRURIA.
ITS FIGHTS AGAINST ROME

In the first book of his Histories, Livy tells us, in a highly coloured account, of the expulsion of the Tarquins from Rome. In spite of conquests abroad and in spite of the public works carried out during his reign, Tarquin the Proud, a proud and violent tyrant, was detested by the Roman people. Urged on by a violent passion, he dared assault Lucretia, an honourable matron who, to escape dishonour, took her own life. A revolutionary movement broke out in which the lead was taken by Lucius Junius Brutus. The tyrant, his wife and children were exiled. In 510 B.C. the Roman republic, which was to last five centuries, was born and the *Comitia centuriata*, the popular assembly of the Roman people, elected the consuls. The departure of the Tarquins is thus described in Roman annals as an essentially political upheaval—as the end of a monarchy based on the rule of one man and the servitude of the citizens. Henceforth power is exercised by its legitimate custodian, the people, and this is the basis of the *libertas*, that infinitely precious possession of the city and its members. Five hundred years will have to elapse before a new personal régime—first that of a Caesar, then of an Augustus—arises on the ruins of civil wars.

The legendary tradition which thus throws into relief the fundamental change of régime experienced by Rome at the time, omits to mention the true facts behind the Etruscan tyrant's departure. The real cause was not some sort of republican insurrection by the Roman people but, very probably, military defeats, due to the alliance of the Latin peoples and of the city of Cumae against the Etruscans, who had occupied Latium. When Livy then goes on to tell us of the siege of Rome by Porsenna, King of Clusium, this account

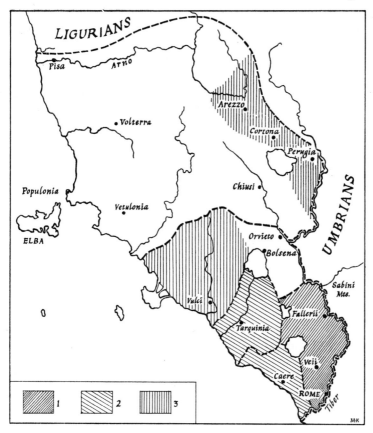

*Fig. 16. Stages in the conquest of Etruria by Rome: (1) First half of the 4th century B.C.
(2) Second half of the 4th century B.C. (3) About 280 B.C.*

undoubtedly conceals the reconquest of the town by Etruscan armies which had brought up reinforcements.

The loss of Rome in the last years of the 6th century B.C. was a grave event for Etruria. It meant the end of Tuscan hegemony over Latium and the beginning of a difficult period in relations between Etruscans and Latins. At the same time,

Fig. 16

direct overland communications with Campania were cut. The period of grandeur of the Etruscans' ephemeral empire is already at an end. In the 5th century failures succeed one another, difficulties multiply and the general setback is reflected in obvious decadence in the industrial and artistic spheres. Everywhere production decreases and its quality falls away. There is nothing on Etruscan soil to correspond to the magnificence of 5th-century Hellenic art, although as we shall see, the classical ideal of Hellas was admittedly not of a nature to find a vigorous response in Tuscan workshops.

Etruria had to fight heavy battles on both land and sea. Rome assumed a more important place in the Latin confederation and its ambitions threatened the territories of the Etruscan kingships closest to it. Veii was naturally the first to be threatened. However, its ally, Fidenae, a small Latin town on the left bank of the Tiber, contained the first onslaught. On sea, matters were more serious. Without land communications with her colonies in Campania, Etruria attempted to retake Cumae and to instal herself on the coast. But this time she was forced to fight alone, for Carthage had just been defeated by the joint forces of Syracuse and Agrigentum. Cumae, on the other hand, received reinforcements from Syracuse and put the Etruscan navy to flight. Hellenism triumphed and Pindar's first Pythic ode celebrates in epic style the success of the Greek offensive. A bronze helmet has been found in Olympia dedicated to the Etruscan Zeus by Hiero and the men of Syracuse.

At the end of the century the situation deteriorated. Campania was threatened by the descent into the plain of those robust mountain-dwellers, the Samnites. Capua was taken by them in 432 B.C., which was a fateful date for the whole of Etruria. At almost the same time, in 425, Fidenae was destroyed by the Roman armies and Veii faced a mortal threat. She held out against an exhausting siege which lasted for ten years. In 396, the Roman dictator, Marcus Furius Camillus, whose fame is justly celebrated by Livy, took the town by storm. Etruria had witnessed with disconcerting indifference the sufferings and the fall of this important city. This lack of national feeling explains the progressive dismemberment of its former empire. The process had already begun in southern Etruria, for Rome advanced to the stronghold of Sutri which was taken by storm.

It was at this point that a previously unknown threat cast fear over both Rome and Etruria. Ancient Italy was in fact undergoing its last great transformation owing to the Celtic invasions which burst into the Po valley and, up to as late as the middle of the 3rd century B.C., made menacing thrusts down the whole peninsula. Ancient authors have left us vivid descriptions of the terror that seized the country at the arrival of these tall warriors, whose customs were still semi-barbaric, and whom nothing seemed able to withstand. According to Livy, the invasion of the Po valley by the Celtic hordes took place between 600 and 400 B.C. But archaeology does not confirm such an early date. Objects from the Celtic tombs of the north of the peninsula indicate that the Celts must have appeared in Italy only about the middle of the 5th century. Successive waves must have arrived between about 450 and 350. This, moreover, is the period when the Celtic peoples, coming from Central Europe, expanded simultaneously westwards into Gaul and eastwards into the Danube valley. The point of departure of the Celts who entered Italy must also have been the Danube valley and Bohemia. The cause of their migration—like that of their kinsmen who set out at almost the same time from east to west—must be sought in the pressure exerted on them by tribes who had come from north and east and whom we group under the name of Germans.

Having crossed the Alps and poured down into the peninsula, the Celts immediately came into collision with the

Etruscans of the Po plain. For the latter—as a little later for the Romans—the new arrivals were barbarians who had emerged from remote northern regions. Their great numbers and their wild cries struck fear into the ranks of their adversaries. They may even have gone into battle entirely naked except for a huge buckler—their only defensive weapon. This martial nudity, which is depicted in some Etruscan bas-reliefs, was not a sign of bravado but an ancient religious rite which we find among many primitive peoples. Individual acts of prowess appealed more to the Celtic warrior than disciplined and orderly combat in the Etruscan or Roman style. During battle, the Celts often broke ranks and challenged to single combat the most valiant of their enemies. They also intoned chants in which they exalted their own courage and cast doubts on that of their foes.

At this period the Etruscan territory in the Po valley ran a grave danger. Melpum is believed to have fallen in 396, the same year as the fall of Veii. Roman tradition, for its part, preserves a lively memory of the terrible defeat which the Celts inflicted on the Romans on the banks of the Allia, a tiny tributary of the Tiber. The legions scattered and the Celts encamped on the Forum in Rome; but they did not succeed in taking the Capitol, which Manlius defended with such heroism. They sacked the town and set it on fire. To make them depart, the Romans had to pay a heavy ransom. It was while this ransom was being weighed out that an insolent Celt threw his sword into the scales and spoke the words which—as Livy tells us—no Roman could bear to hear repeated: *Vae victis!*—woe to the conquered! The battle of the Allia, which undoubtedly took place in the year 381, remained throughout Roman history a sad and humiliating memory. Yet, as far as Rome was concerned, this disaster was to have no sequel. After the departure of the victorious hordes the Romans, who had learned from their cruel experience, hastened to surround their city with a new and stronger wall. But this was not the case with the Etruscan towns of the north, which one after another fell into the hands of the new conquerors. Felsina resisted stubbornly, and fighting went on round it for a long time. It capitulated about 350 B.C. The successive arrival of the Insubrae, the Cenomani, the Boii, the Senoni and the Lingones, finally caused the entire plain to be overrun and, shortly after the middle of the 4th century, the *Etruria Circumpadana*, the Etruscan territory on the Po, had become Cisalpine Gaul. Those Etruscans who had not been able to take refuge in their motherland sought refuge in the Alpine valleys. But the imprint of the Etruscans was to leave a deep mark on the material civilisation of the conquerors.

From this time on, the old Etruscan empire is little more than a memory. Far from being able to dream of conquests as in the past, the Tuscan nation found itself thrust back into the region which had been its cradle; but even there it did not find either tranquillity or peace. The Celts exerted pressure on it from the north; the Greeks dared to nibble at the coast and lay waste its ports. Rome was continually increasing its disturbing pressure and, under the repeated blows of the Roman legions, the kingships, which were so proud of their past, fell one by one. Naturally the Tuscans attempted to profit by occasional favourable periods and launched counter-attacks in an effort to loosen the grip they felt closing round them. They would even ally themselves fleetingly with their fiercest enemies, the Umbrians, the Celts and the Greeks, in an attempt to settle matters once and for all with this Roman republic which they felt was set on destroying them. All these efforts were vain. The Roman conquest advanced slowly but surely towards its goal.

The loss of the Po plain was followed, first, by the loss of Corsica and of Elba. The Syracusans, who no longer went in fear of the Tyrrhenian pirates, came north to snatch away the

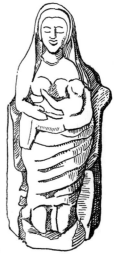

Fig. 17. Votive statuette in terra-cotta of a woman nursing an infant

islands which were of great strategic importance to their Etruscan occupiers. They penetrated deeply into the Adriatic, took Adria and Spina by assault and founded Ancona. On the east and west coasts of the peninsula, the Greeks thus cut the Etruscans' commercial links, the source of their past grandeur. Reduced to a continental state of moderate impor‐ tance, Etruria saw itself forced into purely land fighting, for which it was less well equipped than its Latin rival. Only union and a concentration of all Etruscan forces, which were still considerable, could have kept Rome in check. But Etruria suffered from a malady similar to that which caused the down‐ fall of Greece. The local patriotism of the various cities always led them to put their own interests before those of the nation as a whole. This shortsighted egoism delivered them up to the hammer blows of the Roman legions.

Cerveteri, situated only some twenty‐five miles from Rome, was the first to have to submit. In 351, it left the Etruscan league and as a result Rome allowed it to keep a semblance of autonomy. This new alignment was to spare it the horrors of siege and massacre. At the end of the century, Rome was busy in Apulia and Campania where she was exploiting her superiority. The Etruscans attempted to profit from this situ‐ ation by attacking their enemy, but Quintus Fabius Rullianus struck boldly into the thickly‐wooded territory of southern Etruria, which was so favourable to ambushes, and reached the approaches to Perugia, where he won a resounding victory over large numbers of troops. In 308, the campaign came to an end and Tarquinia had, in its turn, to cede to Rome part of its territory.

It was now that the final phase of this long struggle began. Neither the appearance in 307 of some Etruscan ships in Sicilian waters nor the support given, by an oddly renewed alliance, to Syracuse, which was then besieged by the Car‐ thaginians, should mislead us. Etruria had everywhere lost the initiative and had to fight for its very life. It took part in a vast coalition of Italic peoples, formed when Rome, in 299, was engaged in the third Samnite war. A motley army was formed, embracing in its ranks Samnites, Gauls, Umbrians and Etruscans. But coalition troops rarely have the cohesion of a national army. The discipline of the Roman legions won the day over the numbers of the enemy.

Victory was won in 295 near the little town of Sentinum. Tradition has it that the consul, Publius Decius Mus, offered himself to the Gods of the Underworld and the Earth, at a stage when his men seemed about to be overwhelmed by sheer numbers. This was a very ancient rite of magical origin and with magical powers. By thus dedicating himself to the divinities of the Earth, the Roman at the same time gave them power over his enemies, and the ritual formulae which he pronounced at the moment of his sacrifice also put in Death's power the men whose onslaught he sought to avert. The ancient beliefs of Rome gave an important place to this curious form of sympathetic magic.

The Gaulish alliance was to give Etruria a last opportunity to alarm Rome. The wild tribes advanced south from the Po plain and the Etruscans welcomed them as friends. The consul, Lucius Caecilius Metellus, who came of a famous family, gave battle under the walls of Arezzo against the coalition of Gauls and Etruscans and himself lost his life in the battle. But Roman reinforcements avenged this defeat in a battle near Lake Vadimon. The two last great cities that had managed to preserve their vitality and resources, Vulci and Volsinii, had to sign a harsh peace treaty. Vulci lost its independence and a large part of its territory was annexed. A Roman colony, Cosa, was founded there in 273; this the American School in Rome has excavated since the war.

There remained a single bastion of resistance, ancient Volsinii, powerfully defended by vast walls, which excavations *Plates 6, 7*

Fig. 18. Bronze mirror from Preneste; 3rd century B.C. The Silene Marsyas and a small Pan (Painiscos) are dancing in front of a crater. Inscription in archaic Latin: Vibis Pilipus cailavit (Vibius Philippus caelavit); that is, Vibius Philippus engraved (this mirror). Villa Giulia Museum, Rome

Fig. 33

by the French School at Rome have brought to light in recent years. A slave revolt terrorised the rich and the patricians, who then called Rome to their aid. It was a rash appeal and one which sealed the ruin of their city. The Romans took it by assault, destroyed houses and monuments, and removed the last survivors closer to the lake of Bolsena, to gentle slopes where the Roman town was to arise. In the middle of the 3rd century the struggle ended, and Etruria submitted to Rome. Politically and militarily its rôle was done and it did not even attempt to raise its head when, during the Second

Punic War, the Carthaginian troops under Hannibal came south and threatened Rome. Etruria had been too sorely tried; it remained faithful to its Roman master.

But Tuscany did not lose its personality. Its religious traditions and its traditional crafts continued to flourish until just before the Christian era. For two hundred years its workshops would still produce an immense number of objects which, though of uneven merit, can boast many masterpieces. The Romanisation of the region took place only slowly. The cities of southern Tuscany, being too close to Rome, saw their prosperity decline rapidly. Further north, towns like Chiusi, Perugia, Cortona, Volterra and Arezzo, still enjoyed, under the Roman eagle, industrial and commercial wealth and, in their territories, the richness of the tombs from the Hellenistic period bears comparison with that of the earlier necropoleis.

Fig. 35

In the first century B.C., the bloody struggles between Marius and Sulla had grave consequences for Tuscany and its inhabitants. Several Etruscan towns had sided with Marius; after his victory, Sulla took merciless vengeance. Confiscations ruined the countryside and several military colonies were installed there. From that date the last vestiges of autonomy disappear and the memories of the ancient Etruscan civilisation fade. Yet, throughout the life of the Roman Empire, the people of the region continued to send delegates each year to a religious assembly held near the very holy sanctuary at Voltumna, the *Fanum Voltumnae*, the precise location of which remains a mystery. Thus, down to the end of Roman history, the inhabitants of Etruria would feel themselves bound by the obscure bonds of an ancient national fraternity and by the memory of the great adventure of their ancestors.

CHAPTER VI

Etruscan Institutions and Customs

THE SOCIAL AND POLITICAL ORGANISATION OF THE ETRUSCAN TOWNS

ETRUSCAN CIVILISATION was pre-eminently an urban civilisation, whereas agricultural life predominated among the surrounding Italic peoples. Etruscan history, like that of Greece, was the history of a number of powerful, independent cities which were united by sentiments of fraternity, race and religions, but which never succeeded in forming an effective political unity. Twelve tribes drew their name from their capital cities—for example, the *Volsinienses* from Volsinii and the *Tarquinienses* from Tarquinia—and each of them occupied a piece of territory that was closely dependent on its capital. Rome profited greatly from this state of disunion in the enemy nation.

However, federal ties, which admittedly always remained rather lax, allowed contacts to be established and occasionally common action to be taken. Each year—and on other occasions in the event of an obvious danger—the twelve tribes called a general assembly together at the sanctuary of Voltumna; it was called the *concilium Etruriae*. The list of the twelve metropoleis of Etruria must have changed with the centuries but their number remained fixed until the Roman Empire raised it to fifteen. Towards the middle of the 6th century, it became necessary to form the Etruscan league on the lines of the Ionian confederation of Asia Minor, which also grouped twelve cities about the sanctuary of Diana of Ephesus. The league was essentially religious in character; its political and military activity was merely a derivative and secondary aspect.

The political assembly took place on the occasion of the pan-Etruscan religious festivals; these were held each year and were accompanied by a great fair.

Each year, the league elected a supreme head, who originally bore the title of *rex* (king) and later, in the republican era, that of *sacerdos* (high priest). Under the Roman Empire there also appeared curious figures who acted as federal magistrates and bore the name of *praetor* or *aedilis* of the fifteen nations of Etruria. This was undoubtedly harking back to a vanished past. Did the common institutions that distinguish the Etruscan league reflect on a national scale the institutions of the cities themselves? This attractive hypothesis has often been brilliantly defended; but a parallelism of this kind comes up against serious difficulties as soon as we attempt to interpret the honorific inscriptions of the Etruscans, recalling the careers of the deceased magistrates. The federal bonds of the Etruscans undoubtedly lacked the solidity and rigidity that has been attributed to them. The local patriotism of the Etruscans allowed of only a somewhat loose union, which was insufficient to safeguard the destiny of their empire.

Recent studies have allowed us to understand the political régime in the Etruscan cities and its evolution. Etruscan civilisation was shaped—as we now see more clearly—in collaboration with the other nations of central Italy, and political evolution seems to have followed a similar process. Tuscany, Umbria, Latium and Rome lived through similar crises at very much the same time and the solutions thought out in the various countries cast light upon each other.

Originally the régime in the Etruscan towns was a monarchy of which the Roman royal house of the Tarquins gives us a particularly good example. We have seen that the historians of Rome have preserved for us an exact record of their insignia, titles and powers, which were identical in the Urbs and in the Etruscan kingships. At the end of the 6th century, Etruria, like all the Italic peoples, went through a constitutional crisis. The monarchy gave place to the republic; the king, to regularly elected magistrates. The new constitutions were essentially oligarchic, with annual tenure of office for the magistrates and a stable and powerful senate. All the powers thus passed into the hands of the oligarchy composed of the *principes*, the leading citizens. But the details of the internal organisation escape us. The *ordo principum*, the aristocratic class, controls the interests of the community and seems to delegate part of the executive power to one of its members, the chief citizen. Etruscan inscriptions contain numerous magisterial titles but, unfortunately, it is still very difficult to define their nature and place in the hierarchy. There is much discussion of the relative importance of, and relationships between, such offices as *zilath*, *purthne* and *maru*. None of the solutions so far put forward has been able to obtain unanimous support.

Numerous Etruscan inscriptions, from a relatively late date, allow us to recognise and follow the complicated genealogies of the great families. As in Rome, they are designated by a name—the *nomen gentilicium*—but the Etruscan *gens* is often a very extensive family group and a *cognomen* distinguishes the different branches of the common trunk. Lastly the individual has a first name, which belongs to him alone. The onomastic system is therefore identical with that obtaining in Rome.

Alongside the privileged class a *plebs*, composed of free men and slaves, led a modest and difficult life. From the 7th century on, there were Greek immigrants—both artisans and traders—in the coastal cities. Caere, and later, Spina had complete Hellenic colonies. These Greek immigrants were to occupy the same position in Tuscany as foreign colonists in Hellas. Both in town and country, the Etruscan nobility kept a large number of slaves who were the descendants of the old Umbrian tribes and of prisoners-of-war. When Etruria was tottering under the Roman assaults, these popular masses

Plate 21

Fig. 19. A funerary urn with a young woman reclining upon it. After an engraving by Byres in Hypogea of Tarquinia, *part V, pl. 4*

defied their masters and in Volsinii brutally took power. Such slave revolts are like the explosion of age-old hatreds.

In the frescoes at Tarquinia a whole world of slaves, singers, dancers and flute-players are busy round their masters, who lie nonchalantly on their banqueting couches. They recall a blissful time when the Tuscan aristocracy could count on possessing a picked and elegant retinue. But such works of art must not blind our eyes to the more sombre realities—the misery and oppression which were the lot of those who did not belong to the privileged class or were not protected by them.

Fig. 28
Fig. 6

ECONOMIC AND COMMERCIAL LIFE

Unfortunately such texts and monuments as might cast some light on the economic life of Etruria are somewhat rare and it is only fairly recently that researches have been devoted to this little-known field.

An important passage in Livy (XXVIII, 45) indicates the nature of Etruscan production at the end of the 3rd century B.C. Presumably the various cities of Tuscany were then continuing, at a slower tempo, the exploitation of that wealth which had made them prosperous at an earlier date. In 205, Scipio Africanus was preparing the great expedition that was to enable him to land in force on African soil and deal with Carthage once and for all. The Senate authorised him to accept whatever the allies of Rome could supply for the equipment of his fleet. Here is what the Etruscan cities offered to the Roman general: 'Populonia—iron; Volterra—corn and rigging for the ships; Arezzo—three thousand bucklers, a like

Figs. 20, 39

number of helmets, of Roman or Gaulish javelins and long pikes, to a total of fifty thousand arms, axes, picks, scythes, buckets and oars to equip forty long ships, one hundred bushels of wheat and supplies for the decurions and rowers; Perugia, Chiusi and Rusellae gave pine wood for the construction of the ships and large quantities of wheat.'

This detailed list tells which districts—such as Caere, Chiusi, Perugia—were given over to agriculture or to the exploitation of the vast forests of the Tuscan massifs. Populonia, on the other hand, was clearly an iron-working centre and Arezzo a great industrial city. In fact, all the northern part of Etruria was a mining area, and must have played a rôle of the utmost importance in the economy of the whole country from the earliest times. The metalliferous hills in Vetulonian territory, the rich deposits on the island of Elba,

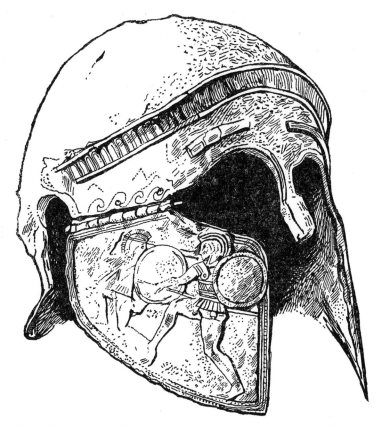

Fig. 20. *Bronze ceremonial helmet, with silver incrustations. On the cheek-pieces, pairs of warriors fighting. From the necropolis at Todi; mid 5th century B.C. Height 11¾ in. Villa Giulia Museum, Rome*

which the men of Populonia had seized, were intensively exploited from the 7th century on and immediately became the source both of jealousy and of great wealth.

The metallurgical activity of the Etruscans was the most intense in all the central Mediterranean. The iron and copper which the Etruscans thus had at their disposal enabled them to forge stout weapons and the superior quality of their armament facilitated their wars of expansion and conquest. From it they also derived all sorts of instruments and tools for the cultivation of the soil and all manner of domestic utensils and objects to beautify the interior of their homes. Bisenzio, on the Lake of Bolsena, was an important centre for the working of metals in ancient times. Perugia possessed famous workshops producing tripods and objects in bronze and forged iron. Vulci was celebrated for its bronze tripods, its candelabra and its weapons.

Plates 33, 34, 44

The extraordinary extent of this work—the extraction and smelting of metals and then, after these preliminary operations, the working of the metals themselves—is clearly revealed by the slag-heaps which are still to be seen at several places in the country round Populonia. As the smelting of ore did not in ancient times allow all the usable metal to be extracted, it has been considered worth while by present-day firms to resume the process. The traveller who passes through this picturesque region of Tuscany should not be surprised to find bulldozers attacking these immense masses of slag which date from ancient times.

The importance of this particular industry casts light on many historical points. It largely explains the constant threats of the Greeks to the northern coast of Tuscany and the rapidity of Etruscan expansion in the 7th and 6th centuries. Internal and external trade benefited greatly from what was in those days an unrivalled currency—raw or wrought metals. Fruitful business relations sprang up between Etruscan sailors and traders on the one hand and Phoenicians, and later Carthaginians, on the other. In exchange for minerals and doubtless for certain Etruscan agricultural products, the Phoenicians and Carthaginians brought their stuffs, their ivories and glassware. Relations with southern Italy, Sicily and Greece proper, were no less active. Etruscan bronzes were greatly prized by the Athenians, and excavations at the Acropolis have brought to light a fragment of a tripod which certainly came from Vulci.

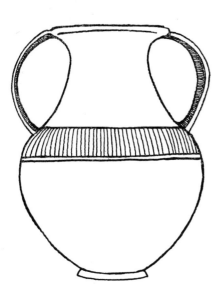

Fig. 21. Bucchero amphora; *7th century B.C., from Cerveteri; Villa Giulia Museum, Rome*

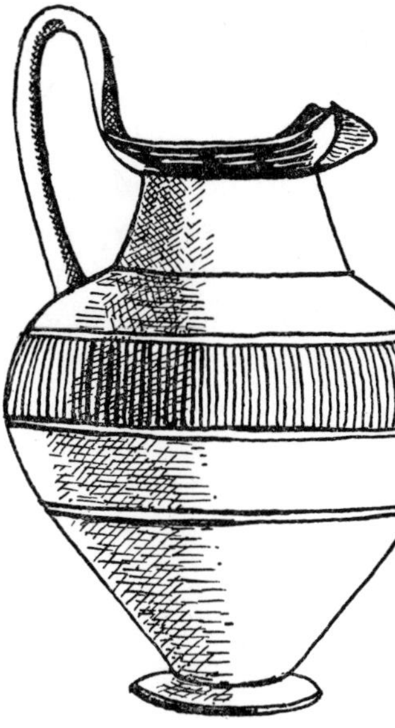

Fig. 22. Bucchero oinochoe; *about 600 B.C., from Cerveteri. Villa Giulia Museum, Rome*

This trade with abroad must have reached its peak in the course of the 7th and, in particular, of the 6th century. It was then that the rich Etruscans deposited beside their dead a mass of vases imported from Greece and, in particular, from Athens. This magnificent pottery, the cause of the crudest errors committed by the scholars of the 18th century, clearly could not be imported without something being given in exchange; what Greece received were objects in wrought iron and bronze and, perhaps, above all, crude ore, which was indispensable for its own workshops.

Etruscan ceramics never achieved the beauty and finish of Greek pottery—hence the craze among the Etruscan aristocrats for the products of the Hellenic potters. However, in the

Plates 72, 74

archaic period, Etruria produced on a vast scale a type of ceramic, easily identifiable by its uniformly black colour and decoration which is either engraved or in relief. This pottery, called *bucchero* by the Italians, is found in various forms which are frequently very elegant, such as cups, goblets, wine-bowls.

Figs. 9–12   It was greatly in demand in Gaul, Spain and in various parts of Central Europe. *Bucchero* ware is found today in excavations stretching from Africa to Britain. Detailed classification of it furnishes valuable information on the routes along which the Etruscan merchants moved.

PRIVATE LIFE AND CUSTOMS

The psychology and soul of a people is nowhere more directly and freely expressed than in the habits of daily life. In seeking therefore, to understand in some measure the minds of exotic or extinct peoples, we quite rightly take an intense interest in their private lives.

Here again the loss of Etruscan literature is clearly irreparable. Where are we to find a more detailed and more authentic picture of men and societies than in the comedies, satires and moral works of all kinds, whose precise aim is to portray them and to bring to light all their follies? If the Greeks and Romans so often seem close and familiar to us it is because their litera-ture, however mutilated it may be, makes them live before our eyes with all their qualities and faults, their fears and hopes.

But, fortunately for Etruria, there is something to offset the sad loss of their writings. The furnishings of her necro-
Figs. 31, 37   polis and tombs provide us with an exact picture of the shape of Etruscan life and its background. The extreme importance they attributed to man's fate beyond the tomb and their belief in an obscure after-life similar to the earthly life, led the Etruscans to construct subterranean dwellings in which to

bury their dead—dwellings that were extremely faithful copies of those in which they had passed their lives. The only difference lay in the solidity and permanence of these sombre edifices. Whereas their houses were made of perishable materials that have not stood up to the attacks of time or the greed of man, the Etruscan hypogea were hollowed out of rock or Plates 15-19 constructed from blocks of stone which withstood all assaults. Thus they easily outlived the centuries and within their impenetrable core preserved the vases, weapons, jewels and objects of all kinds laid beside the dead to accompany them in their other life. All this material was discovered in an extraordinary state of preservation; for, once the tomb had been sealed, neither air nor damp could enter it. We thus find ourselves face to face with the domestic objects used in an Etruscan home. Only perishable materials such as cloth, leather and most of the wood have disappeared, for to preserve them a hot, dry climate like that of Egypt is needed.

Up to this point we have been talking of the inanimate objects used by the Etruscans. But certain of their funerary monuments—in particular the mural frescoes and basreliefs— somehow contrive to breathe real life into our material. For, not content with providing the dead with everything they might need in the world beyond, the Etruscans surrounded them with pictures of banquets, of dances and games, in which Plates 24, 26, 27 they had joined on earth and which they clearly hoped to find in the realm of Hades. These astonishing pictures were not merely intended to call up memories—to evoke the past. No sooner was the tomb closed than, to the Etruscan mind, the scenes must surely in some magical way have come to life and formed the real background to the new existence awaiting the deceased. Thus, funerary paintings and sculptures take us into the very heart of the daily life of a people which in them reveals itself with all its daily and hourly occupations. There is no doubt of the fidelity of the artists who transcribed on stucco or stone the scenes they saw taking place before their eyes. Concrete material details abound in their creations, all of which are vibrant with the profound sense of real life.

The visitor who penetrates into the subterranean chambers of Tarquinia is struck by the sense of liberty and gaiety emanating from the ancient pictures. Men and women are reclining side by side on their banqueting couches, feasting joyously, surrounded by a busy retinue of servants and by male and female dancers who appear to be possessed by a demoniacal rhythm. The various episodes of a happy and unconstrained existence succeed each other on the damp walls of these sombre sepulchres; to the modern tourist that is not the least cause of his astonishment. But the life of the Etruscan aristocrats must clearly have been precisely such a round of luxury and pleasure. Perhaps the ancient writers were right to see in this unduly easy existence the reason for the rapid decline of the Etruscan empire. 'Twice a day,' writes Diodorus Siculus (V, 40), 'sumptuous tables are laid and everything brought that goes with exaggerated luxury—flowers, robes, and numerous silver goblets of various shapes; nor is the number of slaves who are in attendance small. Among them some are distinguished by their beauty, others by the price of their clothes.'

The wife takes part in the feasts and banquets on a footing of complete equality with her husband—we have already said something about the privileged place of the Etruscan woman, and how completely it contrasts with the state of inferiority and even of seclusion which was the Greek wife's fate up to Hellenistic times. The Greeks, and the Romans too, considered such an attitude scandalous and did not spare their attacks on the supposed immorality of the Etruscans. But here it is difficult to distinguish between truth and mere incomprehension of a foreign and often hostile civilisation. Two Greek historians of the 4th century B.C. repeat these scornful or hostile remarks. According to Timaeus, it was the custom

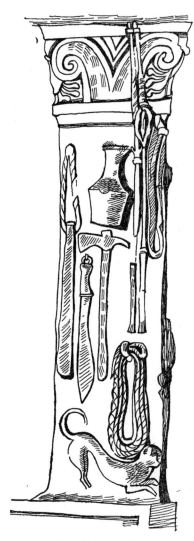

Fig. 23. Pillar from the Tomb of the Bas-Reliefs, Cerveteri; 3rd century B.C. Stucco reliefs show a domestic animal and objects in daily use

Fig. 24. Another pillar from the same tomb

for Etruscans to be waited on by naked servants. According to Theopompus, their women gave themselves indifferently to the first comer and had very vague ideas as to who had fathered their children. Plautus, in his turn, claims in the *Cistellaria* that young Etruscan girls amassed a dowry by openly taking up prostitution. This is a custom that Herodotus attributes to the young girls of Lydia (I. 93). The parallel is obviously very striking. It has been suggested that the Etrus´cans' Lydian descent, which was generally accepted in anti´quity, might have led the Latin playwright to taunt the recent enemies of Rome with this custom. But this very ingenuous hypothesis is far from being proved.

On the frescoes and bas´reliefs the men, in the archaic period, are frequently half´naked. They wear only a sort of embroidered kilt. There is evidence of masculine semi´nudity at this period in many Mediterranean countries. However, the Etruscans borrowed from the Greeks a kind of short tunic or *chiton*, which was brightly coloured. To protect themselves from the cold they used the *tebennos*, a cloak; this was sometimes embroidered or painted, and is the original of the Roman toga. The women are dressed in a tunic which falls to their feet and is made of a light, pleated material. On top they wore a thick cloth cloak of many colours. They seem to have been fond of embroidered stuffs.

Both men and women loved the luxury of shoes. Etruscan shoes were always famous in ancient Italy. They were made of leather or embroidered material. They were long in shape, Plates 45, 46 came up very high at the back and were pointed and curling at the front. They were called *calcei repandi* and were Oriental in origin. Excavations have also brought to light the more common low sandals. The archaic statuettes show a conical coiffeur—a sort of toque of embroidered material, in favour with both men and women. This was called the *tutulus* and the fashion had come from the East. In the colder regions of

*Fig. 25. Bronze mirror. Two ephebes
conversing; 4th century B.C. Louvre,
Paris*

the Po plain they wore a hat with a huge brim which, in
Tuscany, seems to have been reserved for servants and slaves.

Fashions in hair-dressing naturally varied greatly through
the centuries. In early times the men are bearded and have long
hair sometimes falling down to the shoulders. From about
500 B.C. the young men have short hair, like the Greek ephebes,
and are always shaven. On the archaic sarcophagi, the women
have long hair, piled or plaited on the neck and shoulders.
A little later, the hair falls freely in curls on either side of the
face. In the 5th century, it is worn braided round the head;
in the 4th, tight curls once more frame the face. In late times,
the Greek fashion of the chignon, gathered on the neck, was
adopted in Etruria. In the course of these changes of fashion,
the coiffeur of the Etruscans always bears witness to great

Fig. 25

I

Plates 64–71

refinement and elegance. The frescoes seem to show that during the 5th century the women liked to dye their hair blonde.

Jewels always played an important part in Etruscan dress. In the archaic period, the technical virtuosity of the Etruscan gold- and silversmiths enabled them to create jewellery of rare sumptuousness. Some of their work, being awkward in shape, was almost certainly meant only for funerary purposes. Most of it, on the other hand, had served to beautify the living before it was laid beside the dead as presents for the world beyond the tomb. The originality of Etruscan jewellery lies, above all, in the extraordinary technical accomplishment, to a discussion of which we shall shortly turn. The great ladies, naturally, liked to wear such fine products of this most delicate art as fibulae, diadems, bracelets, ear-rings and finger-rings. At certain periods, which are either very late or very early, this display of luxury was excessive and somewhat barbarous. At these times, they did not hesitate to accumulate the richest products of a refined craft. But in the 6th century, representing Etruria's age of achievement, the standard of taste fully corresponded to the beauty of the art.

In the Tuscan tombs we find numerous boxes for cosmetics and spatulae for applying them. These objects had been placed in the delightful bronze coffers that were the toilet and jewel cases of the aristocracy. The Etruscans were reported to have made considerable advances in the art of philtres and medicines. They must also have taken great trouble with the preparation of the cosmetics and dyes, which their women so greatly desired, and which they employed to preserve their beauty.

In spite of the poverty of the sources at our disposal, we can guess that the art of pharmacy and medicine was widely practised in Tuscany. The sons of the enchantress, Circe, who was so expert in the fearsome art of preparing philtres, were said to have become Etruscan princes—at least, that is what Hesiod says in verse 1014 of his *Theogony*. Other Greek authors stress

Fig 26. Terra-cotta votive statuette of swaddled baby. Hellenistic period. Villa Giulia Museum, Rome

the reputation Tuscany enjoyed for the art of preparing medicaments. Such praise coming from the Greeks, who had made
great advances in medicine, is particularly significant. The
Etruscan taste for a very free and very active physical life was
naturally accompanied by skilled research into medicaments
to cure pain and illness. At a time when the art of medicine
was essentially pragmatic in character, they must have been
glad to turn to the cures offered by nature in the shape of
thermal springs. These springs are still one of the principal
sources of the wealth of Tuscany. Many authors in Roman
times mention the healing waters—the *fontes Clusini*, which
must undoubtedly be identified with the still-famous waters
of Chianciano; the *Aquae Populoniae* in which we ought perhaps to recognise the baths of Caldana, near Campiglia
Marittima, and many other watering-places dear to the Roman
public. The Etruscans had certainly anticipated the Romans
in the medicinal use of the thermal waters of their country.
It was undoubtedly from this fact that they derived their
flattering reputation for effective medical treatment.

We know nothing of Etruscan surgery. On the other hand,
excavations have given us direct evidence of their skill in
tending and protecting decayed teeth. Skeletons found in the
tombs of Tarquinia, at Capodimonte on the Lake of Bolsena,
and at Civit^a Castellana, show teeth crowned and bridged
with light gold fittings thanks to the extreme skill of the
Tuscan goldsmiths. This custom must have passed to Rome
under the Tarquins. The laws of the Twelve Tables, which
date from the middle of the 5th century and are only fifty years
later than the expulsion of the Tarquins, specifically forbid
the placing of gold in tombs—except for the gold used to
bridge the teeth of the dead. This is an indication of the pitch
of refinement reached by Etruscan civilisation.

Music, song and games were the favourite pastimes of the
noblemen and their ladies. There is ample evidence of the

*Fig. 27. Terra-cotta vo-
tive statuette of swaddled
baby. Hellenistic period.
Villa Giulia Museum,
Rome*

Fig. 18

Etruscans' great liking for music. One instrument predominated—a double flute, whose shrill sound accompanied religious ceremonies and the various activities of private life
According to the Greek writers the preparation of bread,
wrestling matches and even scourgings, was carried out to the
shrill accompaniment of the flute. This is confirmed by certain
frescoes, such as those in the tomb of the Velii, discovered near
Orvieto. There we see a flautist playing his instrument while
a baker mixes his dough.

Plate 60

According to a curious story by Ælien, a Greek rhetorician,
who lived in the 3rd century B.C., the Etruscan hunters used
the magic power of music on animals. Here is a curious page
from his *History of the Animals* (XII, 46):

> We are told that the Tuscans not only catch deer and
> boars by means of nets and dogs, as is the normal custom
> in the field, but even more frequently by the aid of music.
> This is how they do it. On all sides they set out nets and
> other instruments of the chase to lay traps for the animals.
> A skilful flautist takes up position and plays the purest and
> most harmonious melody. He plays the sweetest airs the
> flute is capable of producing. In the silence and calm the
> sound easily reaches the peaks of the hills, the valleys and
> the woods, and finds its way into the animals' lairs. When
> the sound comes to their ears, they are at first astonished and
> afraid, then they are overcome by the irresistible pleasure of
> the music and, transported, they forget their young and
> their lairs. Yet animals do not like to go far from their
> homes. Yet, as if drawn by some charm, they are forced to
> approach and the power of the melody makes them fall
> into the nets, the victims of music.

The flautist—or to call him by his Latin name, deriving
from the Etruscan, the *subulo*—thus appears to have exercised
a strange power not only on man but on the animal world.

Fig. 28. Funerary urn in stone, showing a ritual dance; end of 6th century B.C. From Chiusi. Chiusi, Museo Civico

His fame went far beyond the frontiers of his own country. Greece and Rome never concealed their admiration for him. We should perhaps see in this taste for the double flute a tradition which had come from the East. In Lydia and Phrygia, the flute was also the favourite musical instrument and accompanied the orgiastic scenes at the religious cere‑monies.

The trumpet also seems to have enjoyed great favour with the Etruscans. It was curved and had a piercing note. Stringed instruments, such as the lyre, which is also represented on the Tarquinian frescoes, must have tempered the strident song of the flutes and the fanfares of the trumpets with its sweeter and more noble tones.

Plate 77

Fig. 28

To the sound of music, singers and dancers enlivened festi, vities and occupied an important place in the religious cere, monies and funeral games held in honour of the dead at the moment of burial. In Etruria, games and dances were ritual in origin and character, as is indeed the case in many other civilisations. Rome herself summoned Etruscan dancers and mimes to appease, with the rhythm of their movements, the angry gods who had let loose that terrible scourge, the plague. According to Livy, this occurred in the year 364 B.C. 'Among other methods for appeasing the divine anger, it is reported that spectacles were invented, which were a novelty to a warrior nation who up to that time had known only games in the circus. Mountebanks from Etruria, dancing to the sound of the flute, executed in the Tuscan manner certain movements, which were not without grace; but they did not accompany them with either songs or actions.' (VII, 2.) These, then, were dancers and mimes, whom the Romans described as *histriones*, a term borrowed from Etruscan.

Their warriors, from an early date, also practised a war dance which had religious and magical value, and was not merely a form of training for combat. It was intended to draw down the attention and goodwill of the gods of war. On the frescoes or sculptured bas,reliefs, we see armed men with helmets executing the steps of a rhythmic dance and beating their lances on their shields in cadence. This Pyrrhic dance recalls the dances which, throughout the history of Rome, the Salii, the warrior priests, performed in honour of Mars. The possibility cannot be excluded that these priests were of Etruscan origin—from Veii, a city near Rome; that, at least. is what Servius claims in his commentary on the *Aeneid*.

The Greeks rightly gave gymnastics and athletics a rôle of the first importance in education. They saw in them one of the best guarantees that the human body would be brought to harmonious perfection, and believed physical beauty and distinction of mind and spirit to be closely connected. In Etruria the games do not seem to have had this elevated moral character. Mirrors and paintings certainly offer us the spectacle of competitive sports and equestrian games. Horse breeding was in favour with the Etruscans who were a body of adroit and experienced horsemen. But certain spectacles have a more bloody and cruel nature. On the frescoes of the Tarquinian tomb of the Augurs there appears, along with a couple of wrestlers, a masked figure called Phersu, who is setting an enormous Molossan hound on a man with his head enveloped in a sack. The unfortunate man is striving to keep off the fierce beast with a club. This strange duel must evidently end in the death of one of the two adversaries. Either the man with the sack will be torn to pieces by the animal or, if he contrives to strike it down with his weapon, Phersu will run a great risk of being put to death in turn. In another part of this extraordinary picture we see another Phersu taking part in a race.

Faced with scenes of this kind, we can more easily understand that the cruel gladiatorial fights may have been borrowed by Rome from Tuscany, either directly—as we are told by Nicholas of Damascus, an historian of the Augustan age—or through Campania. For Rome, these games in the amphitheatre, which under both Republic and Empire, were to arouse in the crowd an unhealthy and never sated passion, were indeed a sad heritage. In the last analysis they derive from the funeral games of Etruria, in the course of which merciless combats between adversaries, who sought desperately to save their lives, were offered to the dead. The blood of the vanquished, spilt on the ground, would for a time comfort and revive the dead who, in their weakness—according to the view of antiquity—needed sacrifices and offerings to restore some of their pristine vigour. The *munera gladiatoria*—the gladiatorial games—were introduced into Rome for the first time in 264 B.C. by the consul Decimus Junius Brutus on the occasion of his father's funeral. But in Rome the funeral character of these inhuman fights later disappeared and the popularity of the games with a crowd whose eternal shame it will be that it found its supreme pleasure at the sight of human bloodshed knew no bounds.

PART FOUR

ASPECTS OF THE ETRUSCAN CIVILISATION

CHAPTER VII

Literature and Religion

IT IS NOT EASY to express an opinion on the literature of
the Etruscans. As we have seen, the literary texts have
disappeared and the epigraphic documents, found here and
there, are still in large part unintelligible. We are thus reduced,
if we wish to judge the literary activity of the Etruscans, to
collecting and examining with care the opinions expressed by
the Greeks and Romans.

The Etruscans do not appear to have had the same tastes and
gift for literature as they had for industry, building, and the
arts. Yet, although they were not a people as gifted in this
field as the Greeks or the Romans—and they were far from
being so—they did have a certain literary prestige. They were
familiar with various works the memory of which is preserved
for us by the ancient writers. Livy tells us that he discovered
from his sources (IX, 36) that, towards the end of the 4th
century B.C., the Roman children learned the Etruscan charac-
ters as, at the beginning of the Empire, they did the Greek
letters. Livy, it is true, was astonished and declares that this is
unlikely. But the evidence is significant and in any case proves
the importance of the Etruscan element at the beginning of
Roman literary activity.

In the world of letters, as in that of the arts, the Etruscans
had to undergo the fertilising influence of Hellas. There are
numerous figured documents, such as sarcophagi, funerary
urns, frescoes, mirrors, coffers and even intaglios, varying
greatly in date and origin, that illustrate various episodes of
Hellenic mythology. The selection used is, in fact, rich in
heroic or divine scenes which we meet nowhere else in ancient
art. We are frequently struck by the knowledge of Greek
mythology assumed by Etruscan art. Mere imitation of Greek

works does not always account for the scenes represented. Etruscan artists and craftsmen lived on familiar terms with the religious universe of Greece. They must have had at their disposal translations or abridged versions of the most widely known works of the Greek mythographers.

In his book on the Latin language (V, 9, 55), Varro quotes the name of an author of Etruscan tragedies, a certain Volnius, who must have lived during the 2nd century B.C., shortly before Varro himself. Such tragedies, written at the height of the Hellenistic period, were doubtless inspired at first hand by Greek works. We do not know what part Tuscan original creation played in them.

Several passages in Horace and Livy mention the Fescennine songs—satirical improvisations dear to the people of Tuscany —the fashion for which passed to Rome at an early stage. Their name undoubtedly comes from Fescennium, a Faliscan town near Falerii, whose exact site we do not know. Here is how Horace describes to us in one of his epistles (II, 1, 139)— a popular and even rustic form of poetry, which had not changed its character in passing from Tuscany to Roman territory:

On feast days (after bringing in their corn) the farmers of old, worthy men and happy with little, relaxed in body and soul. . . . Then with their children and their faithful wives, the companions of their labours, they offered a sacri- fice of a pig to the Earth, milk to Silvanus and flowers and wine to the Genius who is mindful of the brevity of life. Out of this custom there arose the Fescennine licence, which in alternating verses gave vent to rustic witticisms. The pleasant sport which attended this liberty with the returning each year, was well received until the day when the pleasantry, having turned cruel, transformed itself into open rage and with impunity paraded its threats through honourable houses. . . . The poets changed their style out of fear of the stick and were thus obliged to amuse without slandering.

In Rome in the second half of the 2nd century A.D.—so Aulus Gellius tells us in his *Noctes Atticae*—a certain Annianus collected and translated a good number of these songs, the fashion for which cannot have died out.

According to the rather late testimony of Censorinus, Varro in his works quoted certain *Tuscae Historiae*, which doubtless did not date further back than the 4th century B.C. These were chronicles and annals dealing with particular Tuscan towns. The memory of salient events in the life of these cities must have been mingled with the traditions of the ancient aristocratic families. The evidence of the Roman scholar has been confirmed in modern times by the discovery at Tarquinia, the holy city of Etruria, of Latin inscriptions dating from the 1st century, but extolling the fame of Etruscan citizens in days gone by. These are the very late reflexion of ancient family tradition, based on the memory of authentic events and the inevitable exaggeration of families proud of their names. When Verrius Flaccus wrote his *Res tuscae* and the Emperor Claudius, in his zeal for erudition and Etruscology, the twenty books of his lost *Tyrrhenica*, they must have drawn largely on these sources, which not only dated far back but were of immense value.

The most important part of Etruscan literature, and that on which we have the most precise information, was religious in character. These sacred books introduce us into the fascinating and complex domain of Etruscan religion. To this we must now turn.

ETRUSCAN RELIGION

In the West, in antiquity, there was no people more given to rites of all sorts than the Etruscans. This constant attitude of anxiety vis-a-vis the divine powers who regulate the life of man is undoubtedly one of the characteristic traits of this extraordinary nation. The ancient writers also noticed this. The Etruscans are people all the more devoted to religious rites because they excel in the art of performing them, wrote Livy. Very much later, Arnobius still retained the memory of an Etruria which was at once mother and creator of superstitions. In fact all Etruscan life was surrounded by a complicated system of taboos and rules of conduct. There does not seem to have been in Etruria, as was the case in Greece and later in Rome, a gradual separation between religious and secular life.

This fact sets the Etruscans apart from Greek or Roman paganism and their peculiar position is clearly manifest in their attitude to the course of events. To the mind of the Greeks and Romans, the world had, in the course of the centuries, somehow become a normal place. Whereas primitive man conceives of a constant interpenetration of the profane and the sacred, the advance of knowledge had led men to recognise the necessary connection between a large number of phenomena and to understand that their occurrence did not require the intervention of an other-worldly power. This, curiously, does not seem to be the case with the Etruscans for whom, up to the close of their history, all man's actions were surrounded by an aura of holiness. The commonest and most easily explained phenomena in an animate or human nature remained for them indissolubly linked to the presence and constant action of the mysterious forces of Heaven and Hell.

Etruscan religion was a revealed religion. The initial revelation was due to a miraculous being who had emerged from the bowels of the earth. Here is what the legend says: One day, a farmer at Tarquinia, having dug a deeper furrow than usual, saw a tiny spirit emerge from it with the face of a child but the grey hair and wisdom of an old man. At the cries wrung from him in his amazement, everyone in Etruria came running to the spot, and then the Genius, who was called Tages and was the grandson of Jupiter, dictated to the kings of the twelve cities those rules for interpreting omens which were taught to later generations. Having fulfilled his mission Tages disappeared or, according to some sources, died. This wonderful story occurs in Cicero's treatise on divination (II, 23).

According to other authors, part of the Etruscan revelation was due to a nymph, Vegoia or Begoe. She was supposed to have taught a certain number of ritual laws and given man the principles of mensuration and the method of fixing the boundaries of the fields. Her revelations were believed to have been deposited, together with the Sybilline books—the mys/ terious code attributed to the Cumaean sybil—in the temple of Capitoline Jove and then, much later, in the reign of Augustus, in the Temple of Apollo on the Palatine.

In Etruscan times, the body of revelation was handed down in sacred books that were perhaps partly written down at a late date. These prophetic anthologies fell into three series: the *libri haruspicini*, which set forth the art of examining the entrails of the victims and obtaining from them valuable foresight into the future; the *libri fulgurales*, dealing with lightning, its origin, meaning and import, and finally, the *libri rituales*, which are the most comprehensive of all, since they contain the entire body of rules governing the life of men in cities; a whole body of doctrine concerning death and man's fate after death; and, lastly, a complicated system explaining the prodi/ gies which on earth reveal the wishes of the Gods.

This fundamental division of what the Roman writers called the *disciplina etrusca*, brings out an essential point—the

importance of the art of divination in Etruscan religious life.
The theory of thunderstorms, the examination of the victims'
entrails and the analysis of prodigies had no other significance
and aim than to allow them to deduce the wishes of the Gods,
the ceremonies that had to be carried out in order to conciliate
them, and the imminence or otherwise of phenomena endowed
with sacred significance.

We can thus see more clearly the place occupied in Etruscan
life by *Mantike* or divination—that extremely strange and
complicated art which seems always to have been central to
the preoccupations of a people much concerned with the
future and destiny. The Etruscan priests, the *haruspices*, were
skilled technicians who had to master all the rules of a complicated theology. Their original rôle was to take careful note of
the divine signs that had appeared on earth and to draw from
them the practical conclusions as they affected the conduct of
men. The etymology of their name is uncertain and was the
subject of debate among ancient writers. Although the second
part of the word obviously represents the Indo-European root,
which expresses the idea of examination or observation, its
first element has always been thought to be foreign to Latin.
It has been suggested that we should see in it a word related
to the Assyrian *har* which means liver. But this derivation is
still uncertain.

At all events, throughout the history of ancient Italy, the
haruspices were considered, not only in Etruria but in Rome
itself, to be unrivalled masters of the divining art. We have
already noted the curious Oriental affinities revealed by certain
aspects of their technique. Basically, this is due to the Etruscans' constant tendency to read in the book of the world not
only revelations of the past, but forecasts of the future. In a
natural order, in which the sacred was deeply involved, everything was an omen, and a prodigy was itself merely an omen
of particular importance.

Although the Greek mentality was far removed from this constant preoccupation with the future and the gods, divination occupied a very important place in Hellas too. But this common interest must not deceive us. Although divination was very popular in Greece, as the number and popularity of its oracles testify, the Greeks nevertheless adopted an attitude of extreme reserve towards unusual and rationally inexplicable phenomena. Admittedly, the Immortals on Olympus could interrupt the normal course of events by means of prodigies, but generally they respected it, and made known their desires or wishes only in the form of discreet signs—trifling omens which did not infringe the natural laws—or else through the inspired voice of their seers and priestesses.

Their direct interventions on earth were rare—interventions such as the earthquake, thunder and lightning brought about by Apollo to save his sanctuary at Delphi when it was threatened by the impious assaults of the Celtic invaders. Generally, the Greek mind hesitated to imagine the divine beings breaking the regular sequence of events. This takes us a very long way from the Etruscan mentality, which was always prone to discover in phenomena a sign, either peaceful or violent, of divine intervention. Greek philosophy very early took its stand against the belief in occurrences contrary to nature. Heraclitus and Anaxagoras deliberately rejected belief in miracles. Later, Epicurus would do the same, as did his disciples, of whom Lucretius was the most famous. Certain schools, however, such as the Stoic school, admitted the reality and effectiveness of divination. The Greek lower classes were thus inclined to accept the various forms of the supernatural. But the total absence, in Greece, of written ritual laying down specific rules on the subject of divination or on their application, together with the absence of a special college of priests charged with their observance, shows the gulf between the Greek attitude and that of the Etruscans.

Etruria did not share these feelings of uncertainty and reserve; it was passionately interested in the tangible manifestations of the sacred and proud of its college of specialised priests—the *haruspices*—who alone could master and put into practice the complicated instructions contained in the ritual books. How strange was the fate of these priests, who first appear in Italy in the 7th century B.C., at the beginning of Etruscan civilisation, and whom we still find at the end of Roman paganism, holding a place of honour in the suite of the Emperor Julian! They dominated Etruscan religion and therefore intervened on the most varied occasions in the life of the Tuscan people. We must therefore study their lore and rites.

Seneca and Pliny the Elder both describe the essential principles of the Etruscan interpretation of thunder. The Tuscans, writes Pliny (*Natural History*, II, 137–48), divide the sky into sixteen sections. The observer faces South. The sections to the left, in the East, are favourable; those in the West are unfavourable. The sky is thus divided according to the cardinal points of the compass and its various regions are endowed with different attributes. Nine gods have the right to hurl thunderbolts, but Jupiter is entitled to throw three different kinds. There are thus eleven different kinds of thunderbolts. The main thing is to observe the point of departure of lightning and its point of impact. Careful observation of this kind makes exact interpretation possible. Finally, there must be prayers and sacrifices to the gods in order to obtain the fulfilment of promises or the removal of threats.

Plate 78

The doctrine of orientation, which lies behind Etruscan interpretation of thunder and lightning, is fundamental to the art of the *haruspex*. For the Tuscans, the consecrated object is —as it were—an image of the Universe. In the animal offered to the gods, the liver, the seat of life, reflects the state of the world at the moment of sacrifice. On its surface, the priest distinguishes the seat of the gods and, according to the configuration of the parts connected with each god, he can foretell the future. The bronze liver of Piacenza, which is divided into divine compartments in this way, is a microcosm. And the application of the principle of orientation creates a correspondence between the scrutiny of the sky, of the thunder and lightning and of the victim's liver.

This fundamental doctrine of orientation also permits the transference to this earth, where men live, of the image of the sky, the domicile of the gods. The word *templum* is originally a term from the vocabulary of Etruscan divination for a particular area of the sky defined by the priest in which he collects and interprets the omens. During this operation the priest always looks towards the South. By an extension of this concept, the temple designates the place on Earth devoted to the gods, the sanctuary which, in Etruria, usually faces south and represents as it were the projection on to the ground of a sacred zone of the sky. From the depth of their sacred chambers, as from the heavens, Tinia, Uni and Minerva, the namesakes of Jupiter, Juno and Minerva, cast their protective or threatening glances towards the southern part of the world.

Thus, Etruscan thought accords an important place to symbolic and cosmic concepts. In this connection it is curious to recall that the Latin word *mundus* (world), is perhaps of Etruscan origin. Etruscan mirrors show a goddess of the female toilet. Now, in Latin the original meaning of *mundus* is female jewellery and, later is applied to the stars, those jewels of the skies. Its Tuscan derivation seems very likely.

Etruria—and Rome—was familiar with the subterranean *mundus*, a ditch surmounted by a vault, which brought the world of the living into contact with that of the dead. On those days described by the Romans as *religiosi*, the *mundus* at Rome was opened and the infernal spirits ascended to earth through this terrible aperture.

Only a few scant fragments in Latin translations remain on the sacred rules which laid down the application of what was an extremely complicated ritual system. Thus the speech Cicero made in 56 B.C., known as *De Haruspicum responso*, *Concerning the answer of the Haruspices*, is extremely valuable. It presents us with the conclusions arrived at by the *haruspices*, when they were consulted by the Roman state on the subject of a suspicious rumbling in Latium. In fact, throughout the period of the Roman Republic, the Senate called upon the Tuscan priests whenever Rome was excited by particularly grave prodigies which baffled the science of the *pontifices*, the supreme guardians of Roman religious tradition.

The answer given by the experts in Tuscan divination when they were consulted in the year 56 B.C., dealt, according to Cicero, with three points. It revealed, first of all, who the gods were who had manifested their anger by the rumbling sound—namely Jupiter, Saturn, Neptune, the Earth and the *Dii caelestes*, the gods of the sky. It then explained the reason for their anger, namely man's neglect of the various religious rites, the sacrilegious murder of orators and disregard for oaths. Finally, it set out the dangers which the prodigy showed to be imminent and threatening. Rome must fear discord between the nobles and the city—a discord that threatened to put the best of its citizens in peril of death. She must beware of plots against the state and the overthrow of the régime.

The Ciceronian text omits only to recall what was normally the fourth point in the replies of the augurs—that is to say, a statement of the expiatory ceremonies that could appease the gods and arrest the mounting perils. The great privilege of the *haruspices* in Rome, throughout her history, arose from the belief among the common people in the efficacy of their remedies.

This complicated exegesis of a natural phenomenon which Man could not understand recalls, as we have said, the Etruscan almanack which we know in the Greek translation of John Lydus. In it, too, the meaning of the peal of thunder is carefully indicated and the omen varies according to the day or the month. We are tempted to think of the Babylonian rituals which, in the same way, set out the interpretation to be given to the rumbling of the thunder according to the days of the year.

We must still, it is true, explain—as in the case of hepato⁄scopy—the gap in time between a divining technique dating from about 2000 B.C. and a discipline which only manifests itself in Italy from the beginning of the 7th century B.C. The progress of oriental studies seems to reveal an increasing number of intermediary steps. But we await the definitive conclusions of research which is still in progress.

In any event, we will find a very marked tendency among the *haruspices* to interpret omens and prodigies politically. This attitude remains unchanged throughout the history of Etruria and later, of Rome. These priests, who were recruited from the aristocratic class, delighted in inviting whoever consulted them to beware of the internal dissensions in the city, to beware of the disorders that threaten the state and the constitutional bodies that guarantee its equilibrium. Throughout its exis⁄tence, there would be an astonishing consistency in the political orientation of a college which was equally faithful to its aristocratic traditions and to ritual rules carefully collected over the generations. The *haruspices*, who were the guardians of the sacred rules of behaviour, always wished to play the simul⁄taneous rôle of protectors of the established order.

The fragments of the Etruscan *ostentaria*—that is to say the books on the meaning of prodigies—which have been pre⁄served for us by Macrobius, Servius, and Amienus Marcellinus, strike us by the strange and sometimes chidlish nature of the interpretations suggested. A sheep or ram whose fleece is flecked with gold or purple foretells fame and power for the ruler of the city and his progeny. Trees and animals are

divided into opposing categories. On the one hand are those
with favourable omens and, on the other, those with omens
bringing ill luck. The Etruscan discipline makes great play
of this distinction between trees and animals of good, and
those of bad augury. It was as fundamental as that between
the omens drawn from the liver of the victim, which are good
or bad according to the part of the liver under examination,
and those drawn from thunder which are favourable or unfavourable according to the direction from which they had
come.

The division of trees and animals into opposing categories
seems to hold up to human society an image of its own condition. Anything unusual in the *arbores infelices* may presage
a human misfortune; the *arbores felices*, on the contrary, regulate
by the rhythm of their growth the full development of human
beings. The various realms of nature thus seem to be inter-
connected by profound and mysterious ties. But we should
have to make a more detailed analysis if we wished to form
an idea of the incredible complexity of a doctrine which, in
spite of its fundamental inconsistency, liked to parade in the
guise of a real science.

In the Rome of the Tarquins, the *haruspices* naturally had full
citizen rights and practised their art there as they did in the
towns of Tuscany. After the expulsion of the Etruscan tyrants,
the situation changed radically. Rome became once more a
Latin city and religious ideas changed too. The Romans continued to pay great attention to omens and prodigies but they
no longer sought in them precise information concerning the
future. The art of divination was foreign to their realistic and
juridical mind. In their eyes, prodigies merely indicated the
wrath of the gods, and they took all possible steps to appease
that wrath. Nor did omens provide information concerning
the future. By observing the signs given by the sky, by birds
and by the sacred chickens, the augur merely sought to know

whether the gods approved the enterprise on which the Roman state had embarked and whether it could count on their approval. If ratification by the gods was lacking, the enterprise had to be abandoned under penalty of the gravest danger.

If the Romans appealed to the Etruscan *haruspices* when particularly terrifying prodigies appeared, this was merely to ask them how to expiate these prodigies most efficiently, and what the appellants most valued in them was their great skill in purifying the soil of uncleanness. But in Rome the situation changed during the Punic wars. The panic caused by Hannibal's victories gave rise to a new taste for divination. As happens in violent crises, the citizens of Rome felt an overwhelming need to know the future. The absence of augurs of Latin stock made them turn to the *haruspices* whose importance in the city once more increased. They could now put into practice all the subtlety of their art and proclaim to Rome the fate that awaited her. From then on, the vogue for divination never ceased to grow under both Republic and Empire. The growing incredulity of the educated classes did not prevent the mass of the people from turning more and more to prophets and augurs. But Rome always lacked specialists in the oracular art to correspond to the tastes of the day. She therefore constantly turned to individuals of all kinds who had inherited the ancient traditions of divining—to Greek oracles, to *magi* from Iran, to Chaldaean astrologers, to Egyptian priests and, up to the end of the pagan era, to the *haruspices* themselves—in order to find answers to the questions which occupied the people's minds but which they themselves were unable to resolve.

THE GODS AND THE AFTER-LIFE

It is not easy to form a precise picture of the gods who made up the Etruscan Pantheon. We generally know them under the guise of the Greek deities to whom they were partially assimilated. But they must have preserved original charac- teristics not readily discernible in their Hellenic garb.

A late text—it dates from the 5th century A.D. and comes down to us from Martianus Capella—undoubtedly goes back across the centuries to the translations of Etruscan ritual writings which had been set down at the time of Cicero by a scholar called Negidius Figulus. According to Martianus, the Etruscan gods were placed in the following order. Around Jupiter there were the superior gods, the *senatores deorum*. Then came twelve gods who ruled the signs of the Zodiac, and seven gods corresponding to the planets. Finally, there were the gods allotted to the sixteen regions of the sky. Seneca tells us that Jupiter, when he hurls his thunderbolt, can do so either without consulting anyone or else after taking counsel with his fellow gods. This cosmogony shows signs of kinship with that which, according to Diodorus, the Chaldeans handed down from father to son.

The information supplied by Martianus Capella and the inscriptions on the Piacenza liver, which is an accurate pro- jection of the celestial vault, allow us to draw maps of the sky as the Etruscans conceived it. The different gods have well- defined stations in the sky and present to humanity a favourable or terrible aspect according to the position of their zone of power. The principal god of the Etruscans was Tinia, lord of the thunderbolt, the equivalent of Greek Zeus and Roman Jupiter. His name appears four times on the Piacenza liver along with other gods who remain a mystery to us. His wife is Uni, who was assimilated to Hera and Juno. Some Etruscan mirrors show her suckling Hercules, who according to certain inscriptions was her son. Menerva, the Etruscan Minerva, formed with Tinia and Uni a favourable trinity which was introduced to Rome by the Tarquins under the names of Jupiter, Juno and Minerva. This cult of triads, worshipped in triple temples, is very typical of ancient Tuscany. The pre-Hellenic and Anatolian civilisations seem to lie behind these religious concepts.

Fig. 15

Fig. 29. Bronze mirror. Venus and Proserpine quarrel, before Jupiter, over possession of the child Adonis contained in a chest. The names of the gods are in archaic Latin and in different cases: Venos, Diovem, Prosepnai (Venus appeals to Jupiter against Proserpine). Mirror from Preneste, found at Ortebello; 3rd century B.C. Louvre, Paris

The Etruscans, being a seafaring people, had a particular devotion to Nethuns—Neptune, Lord of the Seas. He is armed with a trident and calls to mind the Greek Poseidon. He was rumoured to be the ancestor of the royal house of Veii and was the great god of Vetulonia. Mars, the God of War, was worshipped under the name of Maris; like the Greek Ares he became the lover of the Goddess of Love, Turan, who had the charm of Greek Aphrodite and Roman Venus. The name of Turan comes from the pre-Hellenic root from which the Greek word *turannos* is derived. Turan is therefore literally

Fig. 30

the ruler, the mistress. She appears on a large number of bronze coffers and mirrors in the midst of her retinue of female *genii* and takes her natural place on these lovely objects for the female toilet. Apollo and Artemis, whose names are missing from the Piacenza liver, were nevertheless familiar in Etruria from an early date. The group of statues in terra-cotta produced at the end of the 6th century by the workshop of the sculptor Vulca, which adorned the roof of the great temple at Veii, illustrated the Delphic legend of the fight between Apollo and Heracles for the possession of a doe brought down during a hunt. Thus a purely Hellenic myth furnishes the theme of the masterpiece of archaic Etruscan art.

Fufluns, who corresponds to the Greek Dionysius, was the great god of the town of Populonia, which took its name from him. He carries the thyrsis and is associated with Semele and Ariadne. God of the grape and ivy, he is, as in Greece, the personification of gaiety and overflowing vitality and was early identified with the Bacchus of Magna Graecia who had come north to Tuscany with his mysteries and his dishevelled retinue of bacchantes. The male and female dancers who gyrate in the Tarquinii frescoes to the sound of the flute in gardens full of ivy-clad arbours, may be members of the bacchic brother-hoods and devotees of a god much given to metamorphoses—the powerful Fufluns of Tuscany. This question, however, is still unresolved.

Turms, the Etruscan Hermes, is—particularly in Tuscany—a god connected with funerary rites. He guides the souls of the dead to Hades. Arezzo made a particular cult of him. On Etruscan mirrors of the later period, he assumed the name of the Roman Mercury. Sethlans, the god of Fire was worshipped at Perugia. Etruria always remained divided and numerous gods were closely connected with a particular town or sanc-tuary. There never was a unified Pantheon, common to the whole province, as was the case in Roman Italy. Velchans was

Fig. 30. Bronze mirror. Apollo and Artemis seated side by side; 3rd century B.C. Louv Paris

another God of Fire who also threw thunderbolts. He displays the characteristics of the Greek Hephaistos and of the Roman Vulcan. Populonia, an industrial city which derived its fame and wealth from the smelting and working of metals, struck coins with the effigy of Velchans, patron of smiths. Hercle, the Greek Heracles, became one of the most respected gods of Etruria. There he symbolised strength and martial valour, but was also a powerful god of Water, Springs and the Sea. His unequalled courage enabled him to triumph over the powers of the Underworld. The Etruscan adventurers invoked his protection and chose him as guide on their innumerable warlike expeditions.

Certain mysterious beings symbolised the irrevocable advance of fate. At Volsinii, a nail was driven each year into the wall of a temple dedicated to the Goddess of Fortune Nortia, as a symbol of the irrevocable passage of time. Both nations and individuals had at their disposal a span allotted by fate. The Etruscan nation had been accorded a life of ten centuries; Rome was to have a span of twelve centuries, as had been intimated by the twelve vultures seen by Romulus when the town was founded. The end of each century, which is the dividing line between one generation and another, was marked by celestial prodigies.

We are naturally attracted to a purely Etruscan deity, Voltumna, at whose sanctuary in the territory of Volsinii the only pan-Etruscan meetings and festivals took place. Voltumna seems to have been transferred to Rome in the shape of a youthful god of plant life, Vertumnus. The statue of Vertumnus stood in the Etruscan quarter of Rome, in the *vicus tuscus* and Propertius heard the god say through the lips of his statue: 'A Tuscan of the Tuscans, I do not regret that in the midst of wars I left my Volsinian home.' Rome always provided a welcome for the gods of those nations she wished to eliminate. To ensure the defeat of their enemies, the Roman Senate tactfully invited the gods who protected them to transfer themselves to the Urbs. The enemy warriors, abandoned by their gods, were no longer to be feared and the Roman legionaries, who worshipped them with devotion, were able to bring their enemies to their knees.

Etruscan thought was always haunted by the fate of the dead and the other world. This constant preoccupation gives the Etruscans a particular place among the peoples of the ancient West, and links them strangely to Eastern countries

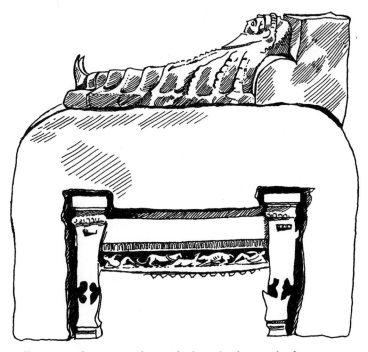

Fig. 31. Small terra-cotta funerary urn, showing the deceased reclining on his funerary couch; end of 6th century B. C. Louvre, Paris

from which tradition made them come. If in Greece and Rome the funerary cult had always been very important, in Etruria, care for the dead seemed constantly to obsess the living. The Etruscan tomb is constructed in the form of the Etruscan house, but with particular care, solidity and lavishness. After the burial, it was protected by a circle of stones or an immense flagstone sealing the entrance against the greed of men and the threat of evil spirits. There the man rested with his weapons, and the women with her jewels. Thus the dead would take pleasure in their last dwelling and not return to haunt the living. Ancient peoples always feared the neglected dead who had become malevolent.

Plates 13, 14   The Tuscan aristocrats constructed tombs designed to shelter the members of the same family. The great *tumuli* at Cerveteri are sepulchres in which the noble families of the city were gathered. The Etruscan necropoleis, whose lay-out aerial photography nowadays helps us to rediscover, did not receive indifferently the descendants of the conquering seafarers and the descendants of vanquished and enslaved tribes. These sombre cities of the dead reflect, beyond death, the aristocratic view of life of a people proud of its race.

Figs. 2, 23, 24   Ideas on the dwelling-place of the dead have always been complicated. Did they live in the spacious chambers of the *hypogeia* or would they meet in a subterranean world which was a pale reflection of the world above? The Etruscans do not appear to have felt the need to reconcile rationally these two differing views. The wine of the libations and the blood of the sacrifices would bring joy to the dead in their tombs but these revivifying substances would also reach them when they descended into a vast cavern in the centre of the globe, forming the collective Hades, in order to meet the other shades.

At all periods, the passage into the other world has always been conceived of and represented as a journey. The innumerable scenes of departure on funerary urns or sarcophagi—departure on foot, on horseback, in vehicles or else in boats—symbolise the journey of the deceased to the infernal regions. The underworld is variously depicted according to the period in question. In the earliest period, the occupations of the dead in the other world are shown in the Tarquinian frescoes to be those of a life of pleasure and joy. The banquets take place in an Elysian atmosphere to the sound of a flute and the guests see move around them elegant dancers and women possessed by the magical rhythm of the dance. The spirits who lead the deceased towards the world from which he will not return, have nothing terrible about them, and everything has an air of calm and harmony.

It is in the 4th century B.C. that the mood of these astonishing pictures gradually changes. The gods who reign over the Underworld now sit enthroned in the midst of their sombre domains, and we can read their names—Aita or Eita, which is a corruption of the Greek Hades, and Phersipnai, an Etruscanised form of Persephone. Aita has his head covered with a wolf's skin, for to the Etruscans the wolf was an animal by its nature connected with the underworld. In his right hand he holds a sceptre round which there twines a serpent. Persephone also holds a royal sceptre and golden diadem encircles her tawny hair.

The scenes represented still have the banquet as their theme. Plates 54, 55, 75
But the atmosphere gradually becomes more sombre. The genii and demons, who seem to be the instruments of the infernal god, no longer have a calm and harmonious appearance. Their faces take on a fearful and horrifying look. A demon who had taken his name from Charon, the Greek boatman, has an important place in late funerary art. He looks very different from the peaceful Greek ferryman who untiringly transports the crowd of shades across the waters of Styx. The Etruscan Charun has grimacing features, a hooked nose and bluish flesh, recalling bodily decomposition. He is armed with a club with which he deals, with a sort of evil pleasure, the mortal blow. There are other demoniacal figures whose aspect is no less repellent. Tuchulcha has horses' ears and a vulture's beak and he brandishes in his hands snakes ready to strike. In one of the latest tombs, in the necropolis at Tarquinia, the tomb of the Typhon—which cannot be earlier than the 2nd century B.C., and which some people attribute to a date near the beginning of our era—a crowd of young people appears in the mural frescoes. This miserable, terrified crowd is led by a genius with snakes in his hair and a torch in his hand. Behind them, looms the terrible figure of Charun.

Thus, in the last days of Etruria we find expressed a sense of fear and even of anguish in face of the miseries and tortures of the other world. With defeat and ruin, the Etruscans had lost their blissful visions of a calm and radiant other life. The terror of infernal torments overwhelms them and the Greek influence is scarcely discernible. Thus, a sombre view of death held sway at the gates of Rome up to the beginning of the Christian era. Perhaps this explains in part the cry of triumph of a Roman poet like Lucretius who exults in liberating man from the senseless fear of an imaginary and unreal world.

CHAPTER VIII

The World of Etruscan Art

THE GREAT ETRUSCAN EXHIBITION which in 1955 excited the interest and the curiosity of a vast general public in Paris, Milan, the Hague, and Zurich where it opened, has drawn the attention of amateurs as well as critics and art historians to the problem of the value of Etruscan art and of its place in ancient Mediterranean art as a whole. The public seems to have been chiefly struck by the unequalled sump/ tuousness of the treasures then exhibited for the first time. Some of the jewels did in fact surpass, in the delicacy of their workmanship, in the richness of their decoration, and in the refinement of their composition, the most exquisite master/ pieces of modern technique.

But the exhibition as a whole presented a picture of an extraordinarily varied art, unequal in quality and composite in nature. Naturally, production spread over so many centuries is normally likely to demonstrate a profound evolution of style and technique and to reveal certain periods when it was less success/ ful. Yet both Greek and Roman collections introduce us to a world where there is a certain continuity of inspiration and form. In Etruscan art, we not only notice numerous, profound changes, but an unevenness which is at first sight surprising.

This has given rise to a number of completely opposed views on the subject. As far back as 1889 the French scholar Martha wrote in a manual of Etruscan art which is still useful in spite of its age: 'Etruscan art had the great misfortune of never having time to form itself.' Certain modern critics, who have in their turn echoed this drastic statement, also conclude that there was a complete lack of originality in Etruscan art; it is, they say, purely provincial and a mere reflection of Greek art, which was its model. An opposing point of view, no less

Fig. 32. Thymiaterion, bronze perfume burner. The stem rests on the statuette of a youth. The three legs are shaped like human legs; 5th century B.C. Villa Giulia Museum, Rome

L

absolute, also finds support among many scholars; namely, that Etruscan art has unique characteristics and can claim to be autochthonous. The standpoint of each side is extreme and therefore partly false. The truth, as is frequently the case, lies in a more subtle view of the matter. Etruscan art admittedly underwent the constant and beneficial influence of artists from Hellas and from Magna Graecia, and its history can only be understood if one takes into account both the existence and the profound influence of Hellenic models. But it does not follow that it is merely a servile imitation, without any real personality of its own. Etruscan art shows trends, gifts and a spirit that represent the achievement of the first people to develop a civilisation worthy of that name in Tuscany.

Plate 61

We can therefore with justice speak of an Etruscan art, provided we do not consider it a sort of entity, outside time and space. We must beware of attempts to construct an unduly abstract aesthetic. The inspiration of the Etruscan workshops varied widely from period to period and from place to place. Artists reacted differently to the external influences of the Near East and Greece according to the century in which they lived and the town that gave them birth.

The particularism of the Etruscan cities manifested itself not only in the political sphere but also in the artistic field. In one place the artists specialised in statuary; in another, they preferred the technique of the bas-relief and the fresco. What is more, the evolution of techniques and styles did not proceed in a straightforward fashion in Etruria as a whole; there were movements, there were startling innovations, followed by prolonged periods of stagnation and backward techniques which varied from reign to reign. Southern Tuscany was more susceptible to Greek models than the North and the interior. It follows that there was a great difference between the various artistic zones; this fact must be taken into account when attempting to date an Etruscan work of art.

A historical view of this nature, which is the pre-condition for a balanced judgment, must first of all consider the very origins of Etruscan art—that is to say, the curious productions of the first Iron Age which is usually called Villanovan. If, from about 700 B.C., genuinely Etruscan workshops began to be active, their work did not lack antecedents; and anyone who has taken part in excavations in Tuscany must have noticed that there is no real hiatus between the production of the 8th and the 7th centuries B.C. Villanovan art is geometrical in inspiration. Bronze or clay vases, weapons and *fibulae* are decorated with simple and monotonous motifs—squares, triangles, swastikas, circles and criss-cross lines. Animal and human figures appear only at a late period and in an astonishingly schematic and primitive form. Sculptures on stone are rare but already show complex influences derived from the Aegean world.

From the 7th century onwards, real Etruscan artistic production emerges in all its brilliance. The great tombs of the 7th century, particularly the Regolini-Galassi tomb at Cerveteri as well as the sumptuous tombs of Preneste, contain material infinitely rich in goldsmith's work and wrought ivory. The greatness of the first Tyrrhenian pirates can be measured by the incredible profusion of exquisitely worked jewels which they offer as gifts to their dead. The preceding period is still present in decoration and ornamentation, in the tendency to schematise and in the characteristic geometrical design; but now we see the first attempt at popular naturalism mingle with a virtuosity that is purely oriental in manner. Innumerable achievements in the minor arts suddenly make Etruscan artists take a leading place among the workshops of the Western Mediterranean. Etruscan art will never shine more brightly than during the archaic period which ended with the expulsion of the Etruscan tyrants from Rome.

ARCHITECTURE

In antiquity, the Etruscans were renowned as architects and engineers of great skill. Rome attributed to them the invention of the *atrium*, of drains and of regular town planning. Roman architects owed much to the information they gleaned from the models of their Tuscan predecessors. Today very little is left of their intense activity as builders. On the ancient sites of the kingships there remain only the vestiges of the powerful outer walls which kept the enemy at bay, the foundations of the sanctuaries and meagre ruins of dwelling-houses. But funerary architecture provides infinitely varied documentation and reconstructs for us the shape of the dwellings which have since disappeared.

Etruscan cities were never built in valleys or on a plain. They developed on escarped plateaux or easily defensible hills; the modern cities which succeeded them still have the look of an eyrie perched on the mountain top and dominating the sur-

Plate 6, 7

rounding countryside. In order to give further protection the Etruscans built strong walls, the line of which closely followed the contours of the hill town. They are of considerable length —often as much as six miles. This gives an idea of the size of the inhabited area. These protecting walls have a massive air, recalling the might of the vanished civilisation. They are built without cement; big blocks of local stone, generally volcanic *tufa*, are laid in a regular pattern. Their size, and their surface shape, whether polygonal or rectangular, is determined by the nature of the material and its potentialities. The Etruscan wall at Perugia, restored in some places and completed in modern times, astonishes us with its truly monumental air.

Carefully sited gates gave access to the interior of the city. They were enormous arches, decorated with sculpture in

Plates 8, 9

relief. Very few of them survive today; however, the Porta

Fig. 33. Ruins of a small triple rock-temple discovered in 1947 in the course of French excavations near Bolsena. Width 56½ ft, length 44 ft

dell' Arco at Volterra and the gates of Martia and Augustus in Perugia are among the most beautiful remains of ancient architecture on Italian soil. The arch and the vault were constantly used in Tuscany and enabled local architects to attempt constructions of a magnitude which the linear construction of the Greeks would not have permitted. At a very early period Rome inherited the essentials of Etruscan technical knowledge; and therein lies the origin and explanation of the monumental character of Roman architecture.

Each city had several sanctuaries where its gods were worshipped. The Etruscan temple stood on a raised base, or *podium*, and was entered only at one end. It consisted of three contiguous and parallel chambers which protected the statues of the divinities and in front had a portico supported by two ranks of columns. It looked massive and squat for it was almost as wide as it was long.

Because of the perishable nature of the materials used, very few remains of the ancient Etruscan temples have survived. Although the *podium* and foundations were made of stone, the whole superstructure was of wood or bricks and has dis-appeared. All that is left, in a few fortunate instances, are the

Plate 10

lower courses of the walls which trace the ground plan of the sanctuary. Excavations have uncovered a large number of decorative elements in terra-cotta which covered and decorated

Plates 42, 47

the wooden parts of the entablure and façade. Antefixes masked the ends of the beams and figured friezes ran all round the upper part of the building. Sometimes, as in the case of the great temple at Veii, life-size statues surmounted the roof and stood out against the sky. In the temples of the Hellenistic epoch, the gables were given groups of statues in relief, repre-senting scenes borrowed from Greek mythology.

Plate 48

All these terra-cotta ornaments formed a plastic decoration which gave to the Etruscan sanctuary a lively and animated air. Antefixes, friezes and statues were gaily painted and the bright light of the Etruscan sky must have brought out bril-liantly the rich range of their colours.

Plate 11

We would know very little of Etruscan domestic architecture were it not for the funerary urns and *ex-voto* in the shape of houses, or for the hut-tombs which faithfully reproduce the design of contemporary dwellings. Researches in the field have discovered only very meagre traces of the private dwellings of the Etruscan aristocrats. However, the ruins uncovered at Marzabotto, a little Etruscan city only 15 miles from Bologna, have laid bare the plan of blocks of houses and of streets. The street system was very regular and has a chessboard pattern. The houses seem modest. There is no certain evidence of the *atrium*, the central room in the Etruscan house, which the Romans took over from them.

Funerary art comes to the aid of scholars at this point. In Plates 15-17 Etruria the tombs reproduce the structure of the houses which have crumbled away. Here the documentation is richly abun/dant. Centuries of excavation carried out either for gain or from love of knowledge, have by no means exhausted the wealth of the Tuscan sub/soil. We must remember that, round a great capital city, necropoleis sprang up, spread and multi/plied for many thousands of years. The taboo on burial places forbade the destruction of any part of the funerary constructions of the past. That is why the largest necropoleis so far uncovered are often only a tiny part of what remains buried in the earth.

To the Etruscan way of thinking, the tomb had to be in a concrete sense the dwelling in which the deceased would con/tinue an obscure and never/ending existence. From the 7th cen/tury B.C. on, therefore, it very naturally came to look like a room. All around the room run the couches on which the dead will be laid out. Then the tomb grows bigger, the number of rooms increases until we have whole houses hollowed out of the *tufa* of the volcanic hills by the Etruscan architects. Until about 400 B.C., the tomb is still of reasonable dimensions, for it is meant only for the family in the strict sense of the word— namely, the head of the family and his immediate relations, wife and children. From the 4th century onwards, the concep/tion is modified and the tomb accommodates twenty or thirty persons—that is to say, the entire *gens* finds a place there. Later still, the sepulchres become almost gigantic; the corridors leading into some tombs, like the François tomb at Vulci, stretch for 90 feet and seem to penetrate into the bowels of the earth.

At all periods, not only is great care taken to make the lay/out of the tombs conform to the dwellings of the living but scrupulous attention is paid to architectural elegance. The ceiling is faithfully reproduced out of carved stone, and we can imagine the complicated system of beams. The frames of the doorways connecting the rooms are elaborately worked. Every, where we admire the elegance of the architectural line—in this the tombs have a real geometric beauty fully in accord to the modern taste for sober art without over-decoration.

ETRUSCAN PAINTING AND SCULPTURE—ITS ARCHAISM

In Etruscan plastic art we are struck both by the scarcity and by the frequently mediocre quality of the sculpture of the bas, reliefs in stone: in Greece, on the other hand, these are always highly successful. The Etruscan artists liked to work in clay and bronze; they excelled in these materials, producing excel, lent results. The scarcity of marble in Etruria is not a sufficient explanation for this strange deficiency. The true reasons un, doubtedly lie deeper. Statuary did not play the same rôle with the Etruscans as with the Greeks and, in spite of contacts between them, the artistic temperament of the two peoples remained very different.

The spirit of ancient Greece is best defined by a sense of humanity and of moderation. Homeric poetry made man the centre of all thought as he was the measure of all things. The Greek gods are made in the image of man. As is the rule at the birth of civilisations, statuary, in its attempt to glorify the gods, took as its basic model the human body. Impelled by a profound, innate feeling for beauty, the Greek sculptor exerted all his powers to produce, by working in marble, the human body in its most harmonious form.

The Etruscans, as we have seen, had very different pre, occupations. Their gods had a mysterious, secret character; Man is constantly a prey to fear of their anger and terror at death. The Etruscan artist had to follow the path dictated by his needs. His duty was to preserve a faithful image of the dead which would perpetuate their features and, in some

degree, snatch them from the realms of night. That is the
origin of the Etruscan portrait. Its beginnings were modest.
In the case of a canopic clay urn from Chiusi, the first step   Plate 28
was merely to affix a bronze mask. Later the lid of the urn is
replaced by a rudely sculptured head while on the vase itself
the breasts are indicated, and the handle, by an odd meta-
morphosis, crudely represents the arms. From this hybrid
collection, which reminds us of primitive or native art, we
pass at length to the statue proper.

The profound influence of Hellenic models would very
quickly make itself felt on a plastic art that was essentially   Plates 29-31
funerary in origin. Because of its stylisation, Greek archaic art
appealed to the Etruscan temperament, seeing that, when
reproducing reality, the Etruscans always preferred a bold,
personal vision to fidelity and harmony. Thus Etruria responded
whole-heartedly to the influences from Hellas and the Greek
colonies in the East. General conditions favoured this artistic
impulse. In the 6th century, Etruria reached its peak of power
and prosperity. That century also saw the apogee of its art.

Attention has naturally been drawn of late to the admirable
group of terra-cotta statues, brought to light at Veii in 1916,
which decorated the roof of the great temple to Apollo. It is
the only plastic group whose context is sufficiently clear to us.   *Fig. 34*
There is no doubt that these exceptional works came from the
workshop of the mastercraftsman Vulca, who—as Pliny tells   Plates 39-41
us—worked on the decoration of the Capitoline temple
shortly before 500 B.C. Although, when dealing with Etruscan
art, we often hesitate to speak of schools, this term is very
properly used in the case of the statues from Veii. At the end
of the 6th century, Veii possessed an excellent school of
sculptors who, while accepting the traditions of Greek archaic
art, used them to produce original work. The Apollo and the
Goddess suckling the child come very close to contemporary
Attic and Ionian statuary. Nevertheless, the gulf that separates

them from the group of *Kores* in the Acropolis is evident. The latter have a divine harmony whereas the Etruscan figures express great inner tension and the artist has striven to render in the most striking possible manner the rhythm of their move, ments and steps. The forms and the folds of the draperies are deliberately stylised and the general aim is to stress the swiftness in action, the dynamism of the deities.

This taste for stylisation and simplification of forms led, in general, to a preference for bas-relief over figures in the round. At the end of the 6th, and in the first part of the 5th centuries, Chiusi saw the creation of an admirable series of bas-reliefs cut in local stone for the decoration of urns or funerary *cippi*. The themes employed show the ceremonies and games which accompanied the funeral; they are at the same time a forecast of the Elysian joys in the life hereafter. The relief is extremely flat and the artist, who did not bother greatly to produce an effect of volume or plasticity, has directed all his efforts towards animating the individual figures and groups. Their move, ments are made to balance each other in skilful symmetry and nothing impedes the rhythm of the race or the dance. Some, times the bodies are consciously deformed—the hands and feet, for instance, are disproportionately long—for the sculptor interprets reality in accordance with his personal vision and the exigencies of the effect desired. The exceptional artistic value of the Chiusi bas-reliefs calls for protracted study. Their supple and sinuous lines have an attractive quality that is sometimes curiously modern.

From an early date the Etruscan took a very lively pleasure in the representation of animals, real or imaginary. This taste was largely inspired by the innumerable models offered by Oriental art and seems to have been extremely popular. The various species represented acquired a precise significance in the rites of the dead. Lions and tigers and such hybrid monsters as sphinxes, chimeras and griffons, effectively protected the

Plate 52

Plates 32, 34–36

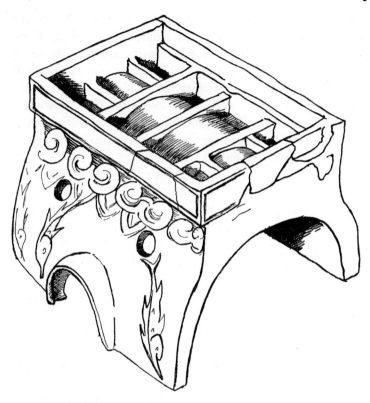

Fig. 34. Terra-cotta plinth found near the temple of Veii. It rested on the ridge of the temple roof and bore one of the statues in the Apollo group

dead, whose doors they guard. The roaring lion recalls a type popular in Asia Minor and Mesopotamia; at this point there seems to be an odd affinity between Etruscan art and the Hittite inspiration.

Large bronzes are the best expression of the animal art of the Etruscans. One of these had a famous history. The cele-brated she-wolf, now in the Capitoline Museum in Rome, dates—like the group of statues from Veii—from the very end of the 6th century B.C. It was removed from Etruria to Rome where it was considered to be the symbol of the Eternal City. After a period of eclipse, which remains a mystery to us, it reappears in the 10th century A.D. and becomes the pride of the Lateran Palace. The two twins who suck at the beast's teats are the work of a Renaissance artist. The she-wolf is tense and wild and calls to mind the style of the workshops at Veii; perhaps neighbouring workshops gave birth to the Apollo and to this immortal bronze.

Plates 20–27
In view of the almost complete destruction of ancient paintings, the frescoes at Tarquinia, Chiusi and Orvieto provide a collection of exceptional interest and value. Easel paintings have almost entirely disappeared; the wood and canvas that served as supports for the pictures have been gradually destroyed by the humidity of the Greek and Italian climates. Only the hot, dry climate of Egypt has preserved a few very average portraits of the Roman period. The pictorial art of antiquity is known to us principally from the Etruscan tombs and from those at Pompeii and Herculaneum. Some fragments of Greek painting, fortuitously preserved, show that in this field, too, Greek art was often without peer. The paintings of Roman Campania are merely a pale imitation of it. Etruscan art with all its archaism, being steeped in Hellenic influence, contrived to set the stamp of its genius on a complicated series of works, which to this day exert a bewitching effect on the beholder.

Here is how D. H. Lawrence enthusiastically wrote, in his book *Etruscan Places*, after visiting the necropolis at Tarquinia:

> There is a haunting quality in the Etruscan representa-
> tions. Those leopards with their long tongues hanging out:
> those flowing hippocampi; those cringing spotted deer,
> struck in flank and neck; they get into the imagination, and
> will not go out. And we see the wavy edge of the sea, the

dolphins curving over, the diver going down clean, the little man climbing up the rock after him so eagerly. Then the men with beards who recline on the banqueting beds: how they hold up the mysterious egg! And the women with the conical head-dress, how strangely they lean forward, with caresses we no longer know! The naked slaves joyfully stoop to the wine-jars. Their nakedness is its own clothing, more easy than drapery. The curves of their limbs show pleasure in life, a pleasure that goes deeper still in the limbs of the dancers, in the big, long hands thrown out and dancing to the very ends of the fingers, a dance that surges from within, like a current in the sea. It is as if the current of some strong different life swept through them, different from our shallow current today: as if they drew their vitality from different depths that we are denied.

Those who have gone down into the painted tombs of Tarquinia will readily understand Lawrence's excitement and may even have experienced it themselves. Nowhere has the Etruscan genius expressed itself more freely and forcefully than in the daring lyricism of these scenes. The gradual deterioration of these artistic documents seems all the more regrettable. It is, however, inevitable. So long as the tombs remained closed the colours, cut off from the air, did not alter and the rare freshness of their hues surprised and enchanted the first men to enter the virgin sepulchres. But once the tomb was opened the harmful action of the damp and the air gradually took toll.

The number of painted tombs discovered up to now is relatively high—more than sixty at Tarquinia, some twenty at Chiusi, as well as a number at Caere, Veii, Orvieto and Vulci. And these are only officially listed tombs. Such vestiges as remain today are unfortunately very small. At Tarquinia there are only twenty tombs in which the frescoes are still decipher-able. At Chiusi, the paintings have almost entirely disappeared.

However, scientific techniques have come to the aid of archaeology in its attempt to save what can be saved. The Institute
for Restoration in Rome, which has both very modern equipment and experienced workers, has in several cases succeeded
in detaching the most gravely damaged frescoes from the walls.
They are then fixed on canvas and carefully restored. Finally
they are placed in museums where they are no longer en-
dangered. An excellent example is the fresco from the Tomb
of the Triclinium, saved by science from imminent and certain
destruction.

The transference to museums of a certain number of funerary
paintings has allowed us to study the technique of the Etruscan
painters at greater leisure. They painted on a fresh *enduit*, which
had previously been applied to the rocky walls of the subterranean chambers. Generally, the outlines and figures had been
sketched by preparatory drawing. The colours employed are
simple and—at least in the early period—few in number, but
their tones are bright and pleasant. Large surfaces are painted
evenly and their juxtaposition produces charming contrast
effects.

The essential quality of this art lies in the study of line and
the quality of the draughtsmanship. Here again we find the
Etruscan taste for the schematic and the stylised, for movement
and life. Admittedly, Greek paintings and vases provided a
great number of models and, in certain cases, the Greek
inspiration becomes so direct and immediate that we can
postulate the presence and collaboration of Greek immigrants.
But the Etruscan temperament finds clear expression in the
artist's indifference to exact anatomy and his pleasure in noting
the concrete details of life.

In the 6th century, Tarquinian painting has the simplicity
and naïveté of archaic art. The palette employed is relatively
poor and is limited to the essential colours. The choice of
themes is wide and varied and scenes of daily life are mixed

with religious and mythological episodes. In the 5th century, the colours become richer and the influence of the red vases from Attica gives subtlety and dexterity to the technique. The subjects, on the other hand, become more uniform and the constantly recurring theme is that of the banquet which is executed on the wall at the back of the tomb and is framed by two scenes of music-making and dancing on the side walls.

FROM THE 5TH CENTURY TO THE END OF THE HELLENIC PERIOD

The 5th and beginning of the 6th centuries are, as we have seen, a period of relative isolation for Etruria. The departure of the Etruscans from Rome and later, the loss of Campania together with the simultaneous threats from Celts, Greeks and Romans, explain why Etruria lost impetus and went into an economic and cultural decline. Relations with Greece and Magna Graecia become less close, with grave consequences on the artistic plane. But, although weakened, relations were not broken off, as has sometimes been maintained. The presence in Etruscan tombs of Greek red vases, dating from the 5th century, is sufficient proof of continuity of contact. Although Greek classical art was neither admired nor imitated in the Etruscan workshops, that was not because they were unfamiliar with it. But the Etruscan artists, being uninterested in anatomical studies and the harmony of forms, were constitutionally unable to appreciate the divine equilibrium of the Greek sculptures of Phidias and his time. They preferred to stick to older models, which satisfied their taste for striking effects and for stylisation. This explains the long survival of archaism in Etruria.

Techniques and inspiration continued to vary from region to region and from city to city. If we are to understand works differing in both style and taste, we must place them in their geographical setting and analyse the frequently complex influences that come together in them. Work in bronze continued to produce masterpieces. The Arezzo Chimaera, which was discovered in the 16th century and is one of the glories of the Archaeological Museum in Florence, is a fantastic animal—a lion with a goat's head on its back and a serpent for tail. This is one of the finest examples of the Etruscans' constant liking for animal art and the representation of monstrous hybrids. It is one of the peaks of ancient bronze art. The perfection of the technique has led some people to think that it came from a Greek hand. But the work is very Etruscan in the extreme complexity of its curving, sinuous lines. At this period, work of high quality in bronze seems to have spread

Plate 53

beyond the boundaries of Etruria itself. It was undoubtedly from a workshop in Umbria that the Todi Mars was derived —a work which gives somewhat provincial expression to the Greek influences of the end of the 5th century. It is now one of the finest pieces in the Vatican.

The tradition of working in clay continued in various centres. The production of terra-cotta images went on—no doubt less intensely, though it could claim masterpieces like the admirable male head from Veii which the Italians, because

Plates 49, 50

of its sullen expression, call 'Malvolta'. Excavations at Tarquinia before the war brought to light a fine group for the frontal decoration of a temple—two winged horses harnessed to the shaft of a chariot which is itself lost. The group is striking in its movement and shows a very sure plastic touch. The work dates from about 300 B.C. and came from the hands of an artist of undisputable power. Meanwhile, to the north of the Appenines, the workshops at Bologna were turning out *steles* with elegant flat reliefs. They were sculptured on soft stone and the scenes depicted display a whole range of funerary symbols.

Fig. 35. Acroteria in the form of a palm-leaf. From the temple dello Scasato at Civita Castellana (Faleri); 3rd century B.C. Villa Giulia Museum, Rome

At the end of the 4th century the Hellenistic period begins, and, with it, production becomes both abundant and very unequal in quality. The Etruscan workshops continue to specialise regionally and locally. This artistic dispersal persisted after the Roman conquest and did not disappear until the end of the first century A.D. Under Roman domination Etruria ceased to have an autonomous rôle or an autonomous personality.

Undoubtedly the execution and finish of the work of this *Figs. 17, 26, 27, 38* late period often leaves much to be desired. Etruscan works can

M

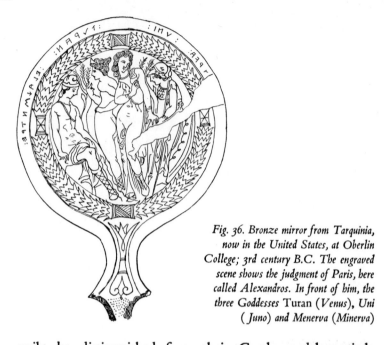

Fig. 36. Bronze mirror from Tarquinia, now in the United States, at Oberlin College; 3rd century B.C. The engraved scene shows the judgment of Paris, here called Alexandros. In front of him, the three Goddesses Turan (Venus), Uni (Juno) and Menerva (Minerva)

easily be distinguished from their Greek models precisely because of their technical inferiority. Yet here and there we find examples of indisputable creative power. The deep-rooted characteristics of Hellenistic art—its taste for the concrete, the picturesque and the dramatic, together with its sensuality—found a ready response in the Etruscan temperament. The Hellenistic models often stimulated works of great daring and real beauty. The torso of the young god which adorned the façade of the temple at Falerii, expresses the somewhat languid grace dear to Greek sculpture at this period. We see in the noble face, with its slightly moody expression, the sensual quality of the Hellenistic portraits. The clay urn from Tuscania, dating from about 100 B.C. and representing the dying Adonis, strikes us by its intensity of expression and—we might almost say—its modern quality. With very simple means the artist

Plate 61

Fig. 37. Head of a young woman called Velia, taking part in a celebration at the side of her husband Arnth Velcha. Fresco from the Tarquinian Tomb of Orcus; end of the 4th century B.C.

has contrived to produce the expression of extreme emotion and to make us feel the dying breath of the young hunter—his last agony in the embrace of death. Our eyes linger on the harmony achieved by repeating the sinuous lines of the ephebe's body in those of the dogs at the foot of the funeral couch and in the heavy folds of the cloth.

Fig. 37

Etruscan painting naturally shows the same tendencies as Etruscan sculpture. The treatment of scenes becomes more dramatic; the composition more contrived and sometimes theatrical. From the Greeks the Etruscan artists learned the effects of *chiaroscuro*, which allowed them to shade their colours and give more relief to their subjects. But it was, above all, the spirit of their art that was changing—the sadness of death, so greatly feared by them, replaces the animated and joyful rhythm of the older frescoes. Some paintings present difficult problems of dating, because we have little knowledge of the chronology of decadent Greek art and this deprives us of pre-cise landmarks. A controversy has recently begun over those great documents of Etruscan paintings, the frescoes from the François tomb at Vulci and those in the Tomb of the Typhon at Tarquinia. The question at issue is whether the former date from about 300 B.C. or from the end of the 2nd century B.C., and the latter from the 2nd century B.C. or from the end of the Roman Republic. Since we have no knowledge of the material in the tombs when they were opened our verdict can rest only on stylistic analysis, which is often subjective and inadequate.

We must not, however, deny the existence of a genuine school of painters and sculptors in the last days of Etruria. The series of Etruscan portraits in wood, clay and bronze, or on painted vases, is sufficient proof that there was a real con-tinuity of inspiration and traditions. Five centuries after the extraordinary canopic urns of Chiusi, we find in these late works the living expression of Italic originality. The existence of an initial impulse which, at the end of the 4th century B.C., derives from the Greek art of portraiture, in no way diminishes the natural vigour and individuality. The Etruscan gift for the concrete and for the individual can finally express itself unhindered. By indicating the essential traits, by using contrasting planes and by adding colour, the artist achieves effects which are astonishingly lively. An excellent example is the fine bronze portrait of a young boy dating from the 3rd century

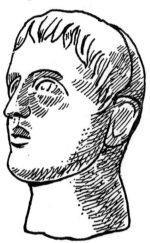

Fig. 38. Votive head in terra-cotta, from Tarquinia; 2nd century B.C.

B.C. and now in Florence. It falls perfectly naturally into place in a series of impressive works and is not unworthy of comparison with the Florentine bronzes of the Renaissance.

Plates 56, 57

The Etruscan portrait is not, therefore, as has sometimes been claimed, merely a peripheral and provincial copy of the Greek portrait but an original creation. It pointed the way to the Roman portrait. It is an art that bears witness to the deep-seated Etruscan leaning towards tough, vital realism—a leaning which, to our eyes, sometimes obscures the Hellenic influence but which, at various periods, expresses itself with the violence of a long contained urge.

The question of the continuing influence of Etruscan art is a fascinating one, but it has not yet been entirely elucidated. The motif of the reclining figure on the Etruscan sarcophagi was adopted by Roman and thereafter by Romanesque and modern art. It would be interesting to determine more exactly the possible influence of certain Etruscan works on the Italian art of the Renaissance.

Plates 49, 50

Certain resemblances are astonishing—for instance, that between Donatello's St. George and the 'Malavolta' head from Veii. The Florentine marble and the Etruscan terra-cotta have certainly a strange air of kinship. The question is whether such resemblances are fortuitous. That is difficult to believe. They are perhaps due—in spite of the separation of two thousand years—to a similarity in temperament in the artists. It is also possible that the Renaissance artists were inspired by Etruscan works which chance brought to their notice close to the place where they were working. We know with what passion the great artists of the Renaissance were driven to study the monuments of antiquity. One particular Michelangelo drawing in Florence must undoubtedly have been made in an Etruscan painted tomb, for it represents the head of Aïta, the god of Avernus, with his wolf's skin, exactly as we see it in the Tarquinian frescoes in the Tomb of Orcus. This direct inspiration from source is undoubtedly the origin of the affinities in details and style between works of art set so far apart in the history of art.

THE MINOR ARTS

Figs. 12, 32, 40, 41

Alongside the great creations in the plastic arts there is an infinite variety of everyday objects. Intended, at the same time, to beautify life, they lead us into a region where the Etruscan genius expressed itself with spontaneity and charm. Little

Fig. 39. Bronze mirror from Preneste, with figure of Gorgon; 2nd century B.C. Villa Giulia Museum, Rome

bronzes, mirrors and engraved coffers, ivories, intaglios and jewels, were all produced with care and taste by workshops using skilled techniques the details of which in some cases still escape us. From the 7th century until the end of the Roman Republic, these little objects are found in great numbers in the tombs. An idea of their variety and richness can be obtained from the great Etruscan museums, where they take pride of place.

Plate 76

Like many Eastern peoples, the Etruscans had a predilection for work in ivory and gold—precious materials permitting the most exquisite effects. The ivory and gold were imported from Africa and Asia to meet the requirements of a refined clientèle. The infinitely rich treasures of the great 7th- and 6th-century tombs give an idea of the luxury which reigned in Etruscan aristocratic society at the height of its power.

From the beginning, Etruscan gold- and silversmiths possessed well tried techniques which doubtless originated in the Caucasus and the countries of the Aegean. Two forms of decoration—filigree and granulation—enabled them to create jewels with a skill and artistry never equalled even in modern times. The craftsman obtained the filigree by drawing the gold, which is very malleable, and thus producing wires of extreme thinness. With these wires he made elegant arabesques on the jewel he was decorating, whether it was a fibula, an ear-ring or a bracelet. Granulation, on the other hand, consisted in reducing the gold to tiny balls, the diameter of which is sometimes no more than two hundredths of a millimetre. Under the microscope these infinitesimal balls reveal extreme fineness and regularity. The most difficult part of the operation was the soldering of the filigree or the granules on to the base of the jewel. This process, which did not alter the shape of the balls or of the wire, was an operation of extreme difficulty and modern workers do not know how the Etruscans contrived to do it. Various explanations have been advanced by the experts and we are approaching an explanation of the mystery.

At all events, the Etruscan goldsmiths in the archaic period produced objects of rare virtuosity and even Greek jewels did not attain such a pitch of perfection. Necklaces, rings, bracelets, agrafes and ear-rings, from the high period of Etruscan civilisation form the most extraordinary series of objects ever produced and, in spite of the interest they arouse, can still not be imitated.

Fig. 40. Bronze statuette of a warrior in combat. 5th century B.C. From Cagli in the Marches. Villa Giulia Museum, Rome.

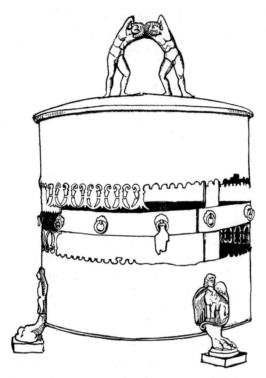

Fig. 41. Bronze coffer with open-work lid. It rests on three lions' claws, each surmounted by a sphinx. From Preneste; second half of 4th century B.C. Villa Giulia Museum, Rome

The Etruscans also excelled in engraving on metal with the burin and the thousands of mirrors and coffers that have come down to us demonstrate the subtle art with which they practised this method of decorating bronze. The ancient mirror is in the shape of a disc of metal, one surface of which, being carefully polished, reflects. The other face is decorated in relief or by incision, but the engraved mirror is common in Etruria. The mirrors and other objects for the toilet or for use as ornaments were kept in elegant bronze coffers, usually cylindrical, but sometimes square or oval in shape. Delicate pieces of sculpture were used as lid-handles or feet. The coffer itself was decorated with a series of etched scenes in the form of a frieze.

These objects of daily use, dear to women, are, in the main, creations of the late period. There are only a few archaic mirrors. Their number increases in the 4th century and during the Hellenic period. It is then that the Etrusco-Latin town of Preneste becomes their main centre of manufacture. The coffers themselves are also nearly all of Preneste origin. Gradu-ally, the mythological or national subjects depicted on them, are reduced to a few themes suitable for such aids to beauty. Youths in conversation, or women hurrying to the fountain; Turan-Venus surrounded by young naked women, her pro-tegées and ladies-in-waiting; Paris hesitating between Juno, Minerva and Venus, his heart already inclining towards the last-named. The elegance and gracefulness of the decoration frequently reflect Hellenic influences, and this familiar world of everyday objects has—perhaps more than the plastic arts—assimilated the harmony of composition so favoured by the Greek artist. Contemporary artists are not above seeking their models in the masterpieces of Etrusco-Greek engraving. So we find etchings of present-day masters once more creating that enchanted world which came to life before the eyes of the fashionable ladies of ancient Etruria.

Plate 79

Figs. 29, 30, 36, 39

Conclusion

WE HAVE SEEN that the domain of Etruscan art is vast and that much still remains to be discovered about it. Meanwhile, one hesitates to express an opinion on certain formalistic aesthetic theories which attempt to define this art by over-rigid formulae. Some deny that it possessed an aesthetic consciousness of its own or even a tradition of style. But that is certainly true neither of all the periods of Etruscan art nor of all forms of Etruscan artistic creation. In my view it is wrong to attempt to consider Etruscan art as an entity and to seek in it, as some say, a fundamental structure. People apparently do not realise that it is inevitably difficult, if not impossible to define in a few formulae an art extending over some seven centuries. Would we not encounter difficulties—perhaps of a less serious nature but fundamentally similar—were we to attempt to characterise in a few words the art of one of the countries of present-day Europe between, let us say, 1200 and 1900?

Our judgment must therefore be more discerning and more subtle, like the art to which we are applying it. Etruscan art, neither completely autonomous nor servilely dependent on Greece, passed through many periods, which differ in quality and creative inspiration. A strong personal vision of the world and of things, a constant tendency towards stylisation of line and form, a pronounced taste for colour, movement and life, impart to its creations an original and sometimes modern look.

Similar care should be taken when passing judgment on the Etruscan people and its astonishing fate. In spite of the mystery surrounding their origins and language, the history of the Etruscans today emerges more clearly as a history rich in changing fortunes and both passive and active influences.

These people were an active civilising agent in the heart of Italy, and their impetus, together with that of the Greek colonisers, released the peninsula from the obscurity of early barbarism. Their civilisation was extremely complex, eastern in its remote origins and strongly Hellenised from the archaic period onwards. They brought Eastern ways of thought and expression to Italian soil, but they also transmitted the art and the religion of Hellas.

Rooted in the soil of Italy, the Etruscans did not have an autonomous or isolated history, but participated in the evolution of the peoples living around them. The true beginnings of Rome are to be found in their presence on the seven hills. Rome rid herself at an early date of the Etruscan tyrants, but she preserved a great part of their heritage. And the hatred Rome bore Etruria for centuries must not lead us to underestimate the importance of the debt owed to Etruria by Rome. The Etruscan influence was to live on in Rome in her Constitution and *mores*, in her religious thought and in the arts; it was to form part of the cultural heritage which Rome, in her turn, would leave to the West.

Critical Bibliography

I GENERAL WORKS

The oldest works are of course out of date, but they allow us to follow the history of Etruscology. The earliest is by Thomas Dempster, *De Etruria Regali libri septem*; it was written between 1616 and 1619 and published in Florence only in 1723–24. Eighteenth-century knowledge is summed up in the *Saggio di lingua etrusca e di altre antiche d'Italia* by the Abbé L. Lanzi (1789). Books dating back about a hundred years are still usable, such as that by G. Dennis, *The Cities and Cemeteries of Etruria*, 2 vols., 3rd ed., London, 1883, and by K. O. Muller and W. Deeke, *Die Etrusker*, 2 vols., Stuttgart, 1877.

The following recent surveys are indispensable: P. Ducati, *Le problème étrusque*, Paris, 1937; M. Pallottino, *Etruscologia*, 3rd ed., Milan, 1955; R. Bloch, *L'art et la civilisation étrusques*; Coll. *Civilisations d'hier et d'aujourd'hui*, Plon, 1955. In January 1957, the review *Historia, Zeitschrift für alte Geschichte*, published an issue devoted entirely to the Etruscans, compiled by a number of experts.

II THE GREAT PROBLEMS

The problem of the origins of the Etruscans was discussed at the 44th General Meeting of the Archaeological Institute of America in New York on 30th December, 1942—v. *American Journal of Archaeology*, XLVII, 1943, pp. 91 et seq. Among those taking part in the discussion were: D. Randall-MacIver (Who were the Etruscans?), E. H. Dohan (Early Etruscan tomb groups), G. M. A. Hanfmann (The evidence of architecture and sculpture), H. M. Koenigswald (The Etruscan language). Most of these scholars followed the Oriental thesis.

The question of Etruscan origins is scientifically presented by M. Pallottino in *L'Origine degli Etruschi*, Rome, 1947. In the last analysis,

Pallottino supports the thesis of autochthony, as does Fr. Altheim, in *Der Ursprung der Etrusker*, Baden-Baden, 1950.

The thesis of a Northern origin is propounded by Pareti in *Le origini etrusche*, Florence, 1926, is out-of-date. The Oriental thesis is defended by P. Ducati in the book mentioned above. In this context there is also the article by A. Paganiol, *Les Etrusques, peuple d'Orient*, in the *Cahiers d'Histoire Mondiale*, vols. 1, 2, October, 1953, pp. 328 et seq.

For the anthropological point of view see G. Sergi, *Die Etrusker und die alten Schädel des Etruskischen Gebietes* in *Archiv für Anthropologie*, XLI, 1915, and Sir Gavin de Beer, *Sur l'origine des Etrusques*, in *Revue des Arts*, 1955, pp. 139–48.

The best studies on the Etruscan language are to be found in two reviews, *Studi Etruschi* and *Glotta*. A summary of knowledge on the subject to date was published twenty years ago by M. Pallottino in *Elementi di lingua etrusca*, Florence, 1936. The excellent manual of Etruscan epigraphy by G. Buonamici, *Epigraphia etrusca*, Florence, 1932, is indispensable. The continuation is awaited of the *Corpus Inscriptum etruscorum*, begun in 1893, which puts at the disposal of scholars the whole body of Etruscan inscriptions, arranged geographically. *The Testimonia linguae etruscae* by M. Pallottino, Florence, 1954, is a collection of the most important texts and ancient glosses.

III   THE HISTORY OF THE ETRUSCAN PEOPLE

The body of Greek or Latin literary texts referring to the Etruscans is collected and translated into Italian by G. Buonamici in *Fonti di storia etrusca*, Florence-Rome, 1939.

A number of studies have been written on the beginnings of Etruscan civilisation in Italy. J. Whatmough gives a good summary in *The Foundations of Roman Italy*, 1937; G. Devoto deals with the civilisation of the Italic, non-Roman Peoples in *Gli antichi Italici*, 2nd ed., Florence, 1951. D. Randall-MacIver draws a picture of central Italy in the First Iron Age in *Villanovans and early Etruscans*, Oxford, 1924, and studies the Iron Age throughout the rest of the peninsula in *The Iron Age in Italy. A study of those aspects of the early civilisations which are neither Villanovan nor Etruscan*, Oxford, 1927. For the question as a whole, see *Italy before the Romans*, Oxford, 1928, by the same author. The complexity of cultural currents in primitive Etruria is well brought out in the important article by Pallottino, *Sulle facies culturali archaiche dell' Etruria*, in *Studi Etruschi*, XIII, 1939, pp. 85 etc.

An overall picture of the history of Etruria is to be found in D. RandallMacIver's *The Etruscans*, Oxford, 1927, and in Pallottino's *Gli Etruschi*, 2nd ed., Rome, 1940. Cf. also *The Etruscans* by M. Pallottino, London, 1955. A. Solari, *Topografia storica dell'Etruria*, Pisa, 1915–20, may be consulted on the topographical distribution of the territories and towns. Institutions and *mores* form the subject of a study by the same author in *La Vita pubblica e privata degli Etruschi*, Florence, 1928.

Attempts have been made to rediscover the essential traits of the constitution of Etruscan cities by going back to inscriptions, and sometimes to the figured arts. Mention must be made in this context of A. Rosenberg's *Der Staat der alten Antiker*, 1913; F. Leifer's *Studien zum antiken AemeterWesen*, in *Klio* (Appendix), 23rd Suppl., 1931; S. Mazzarino's *Dalla Monarchia allo stato repubblicano*, Catania, 1945.

V   RELIGION AND THE ARTS

The fundamental characteristics of Etruscan religious doctrine are well brought out in three essays by C. O. Thulin, *Die etruskische Disziplin*, Göteborg, 1905–9. A. Grenier gives a complete bibliography (up to 1948) and a good picture of religion in *Les religions étrusque et romaine*, coll. Mana, Paris, 1948. Many articles on the gods and heroes may be found in the *Lexikon der griechischen und der römischen Mythologie*, by W. H. Roscher.

Two manuals of Etruscan art are useful, that by P. Ducati, *Storia dell'Arte etrusca*, 2 vols., Florence, 1927—and by G. Q. Giglioli, *L'arte etrusca*, Milan, 1935. J. Martha's very lucid book *L'art étrusque*, Paris, 1889, is partly outofdate. *The Art of the Etruscans*, London, 1955, by M. Pallottino is the modern book on the subject.

There are two fundamental books on the necropoleis: Fr. Von Duhn's *Italische Gräberkunde*, I, 1924, II, 1939, and Ake Akerstrom's *Studien über die etruskischen Gräber*, published by the Swedish Institute in Rome in 1934. Pallottino has produced a model monograph on an Etruscan town in *Tarquinia*, Vol. XXXVI of the *Monumenti antichi dell'Accademia dei Lincei, 1937*.

Systematic use of aerial photography is greatly extending our knowledge of Etruscan necropoleis and towns, see J. S. P. Bradford, *Etruria from the Air* in *Antiquity*, Vol. XXI, June 1947, pp. 74–83.

There is no general work on the whole of Etruscan sculpture. The archaic period is studied by G. Haufmann in *Altetruskische Plastik*, Berlin, 1936; the archaic and classic periods by P. J. Riis in *Tyrrhenika, an archaeological study of the Etruscan sculpture in the archaic and classic periods*, Copenhagen, 1941. Another interesting work by P. J. Riis, dealing with Etruscan art as a whole, is *An Introduction to Etruscan Art*. Copenhagen, 1953.

A. Andren draws a good picture of the decoration of Etruscan temples: *Architectural terracottas from etrusco-italic temples*, published by the Swedish Institute in Rome, 1940. The catalogue of Etruscan urns by E. Brunn and G. Korte, *I rilievi delle urne etrusche*, 3 vols., Rome, 1870–1916, requires revision. Pallottino writes on the studio of Vulca in *La scuola di Vulca*, Rome, 1945.

A certain number of painted tombs are published in the admirable series *Monumenti della pittura antica scoperti in Italia*. The recent book by Pallottino, *La peinture étrusque*, Geneva, 1952, is outstanding for the beauty of its colour reproductions. On antique painting in general, the manual by A. Rumpf, *Malerei und Zeichnung*, Munich, 1953, should be consulted.

There are many specialised articles, but few books on the subject of the minor arts. However, there is, on mirrors, the *Corpus* by E. Gerhard and *Etruskische Spiegel*, 4 vols., Berlin, 1839–69, 5th vol. by Klugmann and Korte, 1897; on gems, A. Furtwängler, *Die Antiken Gemmen*, 3 vols., Berlin, 1900; on vases, J. D. Beazley, *Etruscan Vase-Painting*,

Oxford, 1947; on jewels, E. Coche de la Ferté, *Les bijoux antiques*, coll. '*L'oeil du connoisseur*', Paris, 1956. The works of A. Furtwängler and E. Coche de la Ferté do not only deal with Etruria, but with classical Antiquity in general.

An indispensable working guide is furnished by the catalogue of the Etruscan exhibition in Milan, entitled *Mostra dell'Arte e della civiltà etrusca*, Milan, 2nd ed., 1955. In it, Pallottino and his team sum up our knowledge of Etruscan art.

For the principles of archaeological research see O. G. S. Crawford, *Archaeology in the Field*, 3rd ed., London, 1954. On recent techniques of excavation in Etruria see C. M. Lerici, *Prospezione archeologiche* in the *Rivista di Geofisica applicata*, I, 1955.

SOURCES OF ILLUSTRATIONS

The majority of the line drawings were made by Signor Norberto Antonioni, of Rome, who for more than ten years has worked in close collaboration with me on my excavations at Bolsena. The photographs for Plates 6 and 7 were taken by myself. The other drawings and photo-graphs listed below were provided through the courtesy of the persons and institutions mentioned, to whom I am most grateful.

DRAWINGS: Miss Brenda Bettinson (one of my former pupils, who also painted the gouache reproduced in Plate 19): Figs. 1, 20, 34, 35, 37; M. Claude Hertenberger, Grand Prix de Rome de Gravure: 3, 6, 12, 13, 19, 31–33.

PHOTOGRAPHS: Prof. J. S. P. Bradford: Plates 1–4; Editore Alinari: 5, 22, 23, 36, 51, 54–58, 63, 68, 72, 78; Editore Alterrocca (Terni) 13–18, 24–27; Bulloz (Paris): 29, 38, 43; A. Egger (Cologne): 34, 35, 48, 61, 62; Franceschi (Paris): 12, 31, 32, 37, 42, 49, 52, 64; Editore Leda Capelli: 9; Editore Bromostampa (Turin): 8; Editore Ugo Pugnaini (Florence): 50; Editore Angeli (Terni): 59; Editore Brogi: 27; Curator of Antiquities of Southern Etruria and Latium: 10, 39–41, 72; Curator of Etruscan Antiquities (Florence): 28; The Louvre Laboratory: 66, 67, 71; Photographic Archives of the Vatican Museums: 74; Photographic Department of the Louvre: 46; Photographic Section of the Cabinet des Médailles (Bibliothèque Nationale, Paris): 75; Photo-graphic Archives of Paris: 65, 79; Walter Dräyer, Zurich: 30, 31, 33, 44, 47, 60, 69, 70, 73, 76, 77; Martin Hürlimann, Zurich: 53.

The extract from D. H. Lawrence's *Etruscan Places* (Martin Secker, 1932) on pp. 172–73 is reproduced by kind permission of the Executors, Pearn, Pollinger and Higham Ltd., and the publishers, William Heine-mann, Ltd.

THE PLATES

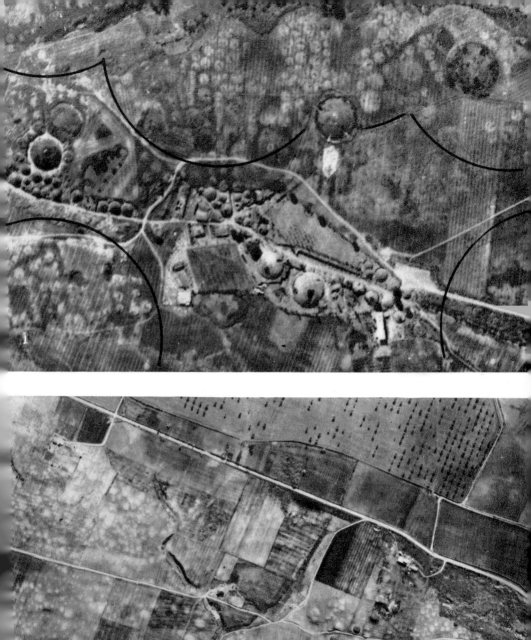

5

6

7

8

9

10

11

13

14

15

16

18

19

21

24

26

27

28

29

31

32

34

35

36

37

38

39

40

41

42

43

44

45   46

47

48

49

50

51

52

53

54

55

56

57

58

60

61

62

63

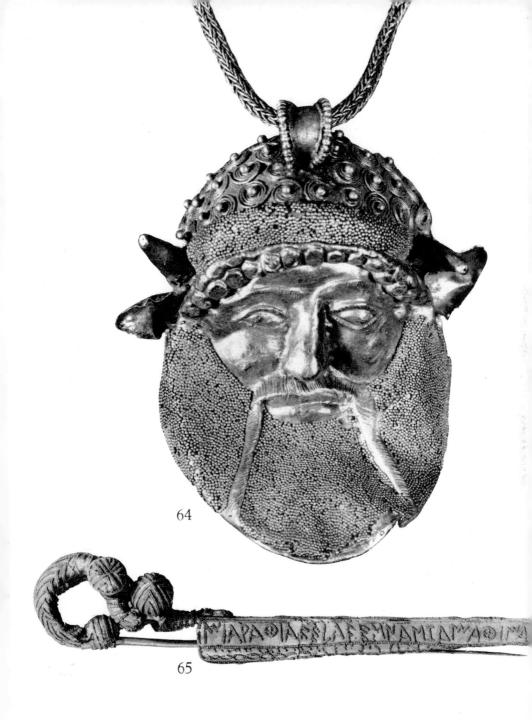

64

65

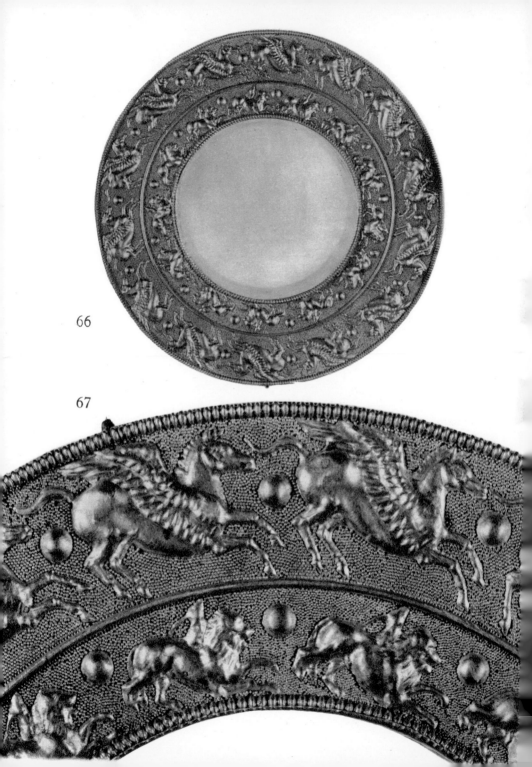

66

67

68

69

70

71

72

73

74

75

76

79

Notes on the Plates

1 Aerial photograph of the central zone of the Cerveteri necropolis. In the
centre, the area already excavated. Between the black lines, little white
patches show the presence of new tumuli. These patches are due to the
grass on top of the site of the tomb drying out in summer. Cf. J. S. P.
Bradford, *Ancient Landscapes, Studies in Field Archaeology*, London, 1957.
Chapter 3, pp. 112 et seq.

2 Aerial photograph of the central zone of the Tarquinia necropolis.
Numerous tombs are indicated by the white patches which are in this
case soil marks due to the mixing of the soil with ancient material from
tumuli which have been levelled.

3 Ground view of the Tarquinia necropolis. The soil marks referred to can
be seen.

4 Ground view of the remains of a levelled tumulus in the Etruscan
necropolis of Colle Pantano. Note the whitish colour of the soil. There
is an excellent commentary on the photographs constituting Plates 1–4
in Professor Bradford's above-mentioned book.

5 City wall of Volterra, in polygonal *opus*. The lower part is a mediaeval
consolidation. On the technique of its construction, see G. Lugli, *La
Technica edilizia romana*, Rome, 1957.

6 City wall of Volsinii—part discovered during the excavations of the
Ecole Française in 1947. The wall, on either side of a fortified angle, is
formed by a double curtain. 4th century B.C. Cf. R. Bloch, 'Volsinies
étrusque et romaine', *Mélanges d'archeologie et d'histoire*, 1950.

N

7 City wall of Volsinii—1957 excavations. (Photograph reproduced for the first time.)   Many blocks have engraved marks which are often those made by the architect to indicate the position the block is to occupy in the wall. The wall as a whole is in *opera quadrata*. (Cf. also Plate 6.) Cf. G. Lugli, op. cit.

8 Wall of Perugia with Etruscan gate. The gate is called *Porta Augusta*. Modern alterations in the upper part of the wall. Second century B.C.

9 Gate known as 'Porta dell' Arco' in the city wall of Volterra.

10 Reproduction in terra-cotta of the pediment of an Etruscan temple. It is a votive offering and must date from about 300 B.C. From Nemi.

11 Urn in the form of a house on a high podium. From Chiusi. Height 2 ft. 8⅝ in. Berlin Museum.

12 Figured capital found in the Campanari tomb, Vulci necropolis. Second century B.C. Heads of young men and women wearing the Phrygian cap alternate in the voluted corners. 17¾ in. high. Florence Archaeological Museum.

13 Funerary road in the Cerveteri necropolis.

14 Little tumuli in the Cerveteri necropolis.

15 Cerveteri necropolis. Interior of the tomb *della Capanna*. Ceiling reproduces pitch of roof.

16 Cerveteri necropolis. Tomb *della Cornice*. Doors and windows have been let into the wall shown here and provide communication between the two chambers of the tomb.

17 Cerveteri necropolis. Tomb *della Casetta*. Chambers opening on to each other.

18 Cerveteri necropolis. Tomb of the Bas-Reliefs. On the walls and pillars of the tomb domestic animals, objects of daily life and, sometimes, demons from Graeco-Etruscan mythology are sculptured in stucco bas-relief.

19 Interior of the Tomb of the Typhon. A central pillar supports the roof of this vast chamber. Tarquinia. First century B.C.

20 Painted plaque known as the *Boccanera* plaque. From Cerveteri. About 550 B.C. Now in the British Museum, London.

21 Painted plaque known as the *Campana* plaque. From Cerveteri. Two bearded men are seated face to face on folding stools. One has a sceptre. Above, to the right, a small winged figure flies towards him. Last quarter of 6th century B.C. Louvre, Paris.

22 Another plaque—same origin and date. A bearded man wearing a short tunic armed with bow and arrow precedes a young winged figure similarly clad and carrying a young woman in his arms. More likely to be a mythological scene than a piece of funerary symbolism.

23 Another plaque—same origin and date. Three figures moving towards the right. A woman holds a branch between two warriors.

24 Fresco from the Tomb of the Funeral Couch, Tarquinia. About 460 B.C. Ephebe taming a horse.

25 Fresco from the recently discovered chamber in the Tomb of Orcus, Tarquinia. Second century B.C. Head of the Lord of the Underworld, Hades, wearing a wolf skin. For all these frescoes, cf. M. Pallottino, *Etruscan Painting*, ed. Skira, Geneva, 1952.

26 Painting from the Tomb of the Augurs, Tarquinia. About 530 B.C. An umpire hastens towards the game and looks back to a young servant telling him to hurry. A second little slave in a hood is crouching on the ground.

27 Fresco from the Tomb of the Leopards, Tarquinia. First quarter of 5th century B.C.

28 Head of stone statue of woman from the tumulus *della Pietrera* at Vetulonia. End of 7th century B.C. First example of large-scale funerary statuary. Height 11 in. Now in the Florence Archaeological Museum.

29 Terra-cotta statuette of seated man, from Cerveteri. Found with two statuettes of women of the same kind, now in the British Museum. End of 7th century B.C. Height 18½ in. Museo dei Conservatori, Rome.

30 Biconical urn in fired red clay, used as an ossuary. Villanovian type. Decorated with reliefs of geometrical and swastika designs. Reveals primitive attempts at plastic art. On the handle, there is a seated figure; on the lid, a man sitting at a table, a woman standing facing him, beside them a large wine-bowl. It depicts a banquet scene in which the deceased takes part. From Montescudaio, near Volterra. Beginning of 7th century B.C. Height of urn 25¼ in. Height of figures on lid 5⅛ in.

31 Centaur in *nenfro*. Massive youthful body with hindquarters of horse. Gives an impression of brute strength. Daedalic influence. The monster was probably the guardian of a tomb. From Vulci. Beginning of 6th century B.C. Height 30¼ in. Length 31½ in. Villa Giulia Museum, Rome.

32 Lion in *nenfro*. From Vulci. Second half of 6th century B.C. Height 31½ in. Length 3 ft. 6½ in. Florence Archaeological Museum.

33 Support (base), decorated with reliefs, of a bronze tripod known as the 'Loeb tripod'. Three scenes superimposed: *above*, a seated chimaera; *centre*, Perseus, pursued by the Gorgons, fleeing with the covered head of Medusa, as Athene shields him with her outspread cloak; *below*, two warriors fighting over the body of a fallen comrade. Bronze School of Perugia with Asiatic influence from Ionia. From San Valentino, near Perugia. About 540 B.C. Height 36⅝ in. Antikensammlungen, Munich.

34 Little bronze lion from Castel San Mariano, near Perugia. Second half of 6th century B.C. Height 2 ft. 6 in. Munich Museum.

35 Bronze he-goat in extraordinarily life-like pose. Undoubtedly the handle of a vase. From Bibbona, near Leghorn. About 500 B.C. Height 10¼ in. Florence Archaeological Museum.

36 Fine stone sphinx from Poggio Gaiella, Chiusi. Beginning of 5th century B.C. Museo Civico.

37 Funerary stele with figure of warrior in *pietra serena*. An inscription gives the deceased's name, *Larth Ninie*. Ionian influence. From Fiesole. About 520 B.C. Height 4 ft. 7 in. Florence Archaeological Museum.

38 Detail of great terra-cotta sarcophagus, from Cerveteri. A husband reclining beside his wife. About 520 B.C. Louvre, Paris.

39 The slaughtered doe. In terra-cotta. Formed part of the Apollo group. Apollo and Heracles quarrelled over this trophy of the chase.

40 Statue of woman with a child in her arms. Found at Veii during the excavations of Portonaccio. Perhaps by a follower of Vulca. About 500 B.C. This statue decorated the roof crest of the temple as did all the figures from the Apollo group.

41 The Veii Apollo. A major example of Etruscan sculpture, undoubtedly the work of the great Etruscan sculptor Vulca. About 500 B.C. Museum of the Villa Giulia, Rome.

42 Delightful antefix with maenad's face. Decorated the roof of the temple at Veii. The face is charmingly framed by a shell, divided by what appear to be rays. Height 17¾ in. Width 16⅞ in. Nos. 39, 40, 41, 42 are in the Museum of the Villa Giulia, Rome.

43 Funerary stele with reliefs. Above, a serpent fighting a sea-horse. In the middle, the last journey of the dead woman in a horse-drawn vehicle. Below, she is received by a winged demon. From Bologna. First half of 4th century B.C. Height 4 ft. 9 in. Bologna Museum.

44 Bronze plate, decorated with reliefs in repoussé and forming part of the outer covering of a chariot. The Gorgon, seated with legs wide apart, holds off two lions with her hands, her arms outstretched. On the right, a sea-horse and a heron are shown. Style similar to that of the 'Loeb tripod', but more animated. From Castel San Mariano, near Perugia. About 540–530 B.C. Height 16⅝ in. Width 23½ in. Antikensammlungen Munich.

45, 46 Little bronzes of young women or goddesses, wearing the *tutulus*, a pointed hat. Beginning of 5th century B.C. Height 7⅞ in. Louvre, Paris.

47 Antefix of Silenus mask. Terra-cotta. The face of the demon is striking because of its rare expressive qualities. Probably from Veii. About 500 B.C. Height 11½ in.

48 Terra-cotta head of bald bearded man. Expression violently naturalistic. From the temple of the Belvedere at Orvieto. First half of 4th century B.C. Height 6¼ in.

49   Fine terra-cotta head, called the 'Malvolta' head, found at Veii. Second half of 5th century B.C. Height 6¾ in. Museum of the Villa Giulia, Rome.

50   Head of Donatello's St George, which has a curious resemblance to the 'Malvolta' head. Problem of influence of Etruscan on Renaissance Art.

51   The Arezzo Chimaera, one of the most famous Etruscan bronzes, dis- covered in the middle of the 16th century. 5th century B.C. Height 2 ft. 7½ in. Florence Archaeological Museum.

52   Funerary *cippus* decorated with reliefs of a chariot race, each chariot drawn by three horses. Probably refers to the funeral games for the de- ceased. Fine sculpture from Chiusi from the period of late archaism. About 470 B.C. Height 12¼ in. Length 2 ft. 7½ in. Palermo Museum.

53   Bronze statue of a warrior—the so-called Todi Mars. One of the few large Italic bronzes which have come down to us. Influence of Greek sculpture of the beginning of the 4th century, but local work. Dedicatory inscrip- tion on the cuirass in Umbrian. From Todi. 4th century B.C. Height 4 ft. 8 in. Vatican Museum.

54   Terra-cotta masks of demons. 4th century B.C. Orvieto. Faina Museum.

55   Sarcophagus with frescoes from Terre San Severo. On each side of this large sarcophagus—height 2 ft. 7½ in., length 6 ft. 10½ in.—are bas-reliefs, still coloured, of mythological scenes dealing with the other world. The photographs show Ulysses threatening Circe with his sword; on the two sides his companions are already half changed into beasts. In the pediment, the head of Achelous framed by two reclining demons. About 300 B.C. Orvieto. Museo dell'Opera del Duomo.

56, 57   Bronze portrait of young man, which is alone sufficient proof that the Etruscan art of the portrait can rise to great heights. Obviously an extra-ordinary likeness, with great sweetness of expression. Third century B.C. Height 9 in. Florence Archaeological Museum.

58   Bronze statuette of child holding a bird in his right hand. Found near Lake Trasimene. Second century B.C. Vatican Museum.

59   Two winged horses—fragment of a terra-cotta group which decorated the pediment of a temple in Tarquinia. The two eager animals were harnessed to the chariot of a god. About 300 B.C. Height 3 ft. 9 in. Length 4 ft. 1 in. Tarquinia Museum.

60   Bone plaque, decorated with reliefs depicting a young man with a ram in his arms. It is a carving intended for furniture decoration. Ionian influence. From Castel San Mariano, near Perugia. About 540 B.C. Height 3⅜ in. Perugia Museum.

61   Part of a painted terra-cotta statue of a young god. Decorated the pediment of the temple *dello Scasato* at Faleri (Civita castellana). Third–2nd centuries B.C. Height 2 ft. 1½ in. Museum of the Villa Giulia, Rome.

62   Part of a terra-cotta sarcophagus. A dolphin is shown in relief. From Tuscania. Second century B.C. Height 15¾ in. Length 2 ft. 9 in. Florence Archaeological Museum.

63   Urn of *Arnth Velimnes Aules*, lying on his bed. Two funerary demons or *lases* mount guard in front of the lower part of the monument as if protecting the gates of the Other World. Tomb of the Volumni, near Perugia. 2nd century B.C.

64   Gold pendant. In form of a mask of Achelous. Hair and beard in granulation; face in repoussé work. About 500 B.C. Height 1⅝ in.

65 Gold fibula richly decorated with granulation. On the clasp an Etruscan inscription. From Chiusi. Seventh century B.C. 4⅜in long. Louvre, Paris.

66, Flat gold ring, surrounding a bottle-holder. No. 67 is an enlargement of
67 a detail of the ring. (Both these fine photographs come from the workshop of the Louvre.) The ring is surrounded by two friezes of chimaeras and winged horses surrounded by a granulated background. About 500 B.C. Diameter 5⅞ in. Louvre, Paris.

68 Bronze candelabra. One of the finest works of Etruscan relief. It has 16 holders. This shows the lower part with a gorgon mask in the centre. The holders are ornamented with alternating figures of a Silenus and sirens. From Cortona. Second half of 5th century B.C. Diameter 23 in. Museo dell'Accademia Etrusca, Cortona.

69 Detail of a rectangular gold clasp. Mounted on two transverse rods, and one central vertical rod, this extraordinary jewel has its entire surface covered with lions and mythological creatures (sphinxes, harpies, chimaeras). The figurines are worked in repoussé and decorated in granulation. From the Bernardini tomb in Palestrina. End of 7th century B.C. Length 6¾ in. Width 2¾ in. Pigorini Museum, Rome.

70 Gold bracelet (or large ear-ring, according to a recent interpretation in *Acme*, V, 1952, by C. Albizzati and A. Stenico—*pp. 594 et seq.*). A similar specimen found in the same tomb. On the band of rolled gold, a succession of small rectangular panels, each depicting three deities of somewhat Oriental type. On the edges, geometrical designs. Entire decoration in granulation. At both ends, on small folding strips, a goddess is depicted surrounded by lions. From the Regolini Galassi tomb at Cerveteri. About 650 B.C. Curved length 10¼ in. Width 2¾ in. Vatican Museum.

71 Ear-ring in the shape of a little cask. Decorated in filigree and granulation. End of 6th century B.C. Louvre, Paris.

72 *Bucchero* amphora, with an incised alphabet and Etruscan inscription. From Formello, near Veii. About 600 B.C. Museum of the Villa Giulia, Rome.

73 *Bucchero* vessel in the shape of a bird with a human head. There are incisions on the beard and wings. The hair arranged in layers connotes a Greek daedalic influence. From Vulci. First half of 6th century B.C. Height 9½ in. Diameter 8⅝ in. Celle.

74 *Bucchero* vase. On the base an engraved alphabet. On the belly a syllabary. From Cerveteri. Height 6¾ in. Vatican Museum.

75 Wine-bowl in the form of a chalice, painted with red figures. Achilles, here erroneously called Ajax, cuts the throat of a Trojan prisoner in the presence of Charun. From Vulci. Fourth century B.C. Cabinet des Médailles, Bibliothèque Nationale, Paris.

76 Gold goblet. This *skyphos* of pure and temperate line has as sole orna-mentation two figurines of sphinxes on each handle. From the Bernardini tomb in Palestrina. Second half of 7th century B.C. Pigorini Museum, Rome.

77 Small impasto receptacle with figurines of dancers on the rim. Carved in the round, the figurines, representing two young girls, kneel facing opposite directions, their hands touching their heads. Ionian-Etruscan art. From southern Etruria (Castellani Collection). End of 6th century B.C. Height of basin 2⅞ in. Figurines 6 in.

78 Bronze mirror from Vulci. Chalcas examining the liver of a victim. About 400 B.C. Vatican Museum.

79 Coffer from Preneste. In bronze, with engravings. The two statuettes of ephebes on the lid serve as a handle. Hellenistic art. Louvre, Paris.

Index